When the Ground Shifts

When the Ground Shifts:
Betrayal, Recovery, and Long Work of Repair
by Marcus N. Tanner, Ph.D.

When the Ground Shifts:
Betrayal, Recovery, and the Long Work of Repair

Cover design by HealingChoice Publishing

ISBN (eBook): 978-1-7372239-4-8
ISBN (Paperback): 978-1-7372239-2-4
ISBN (Hardcover): 978-1-7372239-3-1
Printed in the United States of America
HealingChoice Publishing
Lubbock, Texas

Contents

Introduction

This book began, as most books about serious things begin, with people who were suffering. They came into therapy offices and sat across from clinicians who had been trained to help. They came into pastoral counseling rooms and sat across from ministers who had been trained to care. They picked up books with titles that promised answers. They searched online at two in the morning when the thoughts would not stop. They reached, sometimes, for faith communities that had not been prepared to receive what they were carrying. And they found, often enough to matter, that the tools available to them were not quite equal to what had happened.

Some of the tools were too thin, practical advice about communication and forgiveness that treated the injury as a relational difficulty rather than a trauma. Some were too directive, telling wounded people what to decide before they had the information their decisions required. Some were too clinical for the faith-shaped people in the room, and some were too faith-shaped for the clinically oriented. And almost none of them spoke directly about the experience that most betrayed spouses describe in the early weeks: the floor-has-disappeared sensation, the inability to trust their own perceptions, the simultaneous experience of loving someone and not knowing who that person is. This book is an attempt to do something different.

* * *

It is written for you, the person who has been betrayed. Not for your partner, though some of what is here may be useful for your partner to read. Not primarily for the therapist or pastor working with you, though I hope it will support that work. It is written for the person sitting with the knowledge that something happened that should not have happened, in a relationship that was supposed to be safe, by a person who promised to be trustworthy.

That person is you, and you deserve a resource that takes your experience seriously, which means, among other things, not asking you to move faster than your nervous system can move, not insisting on outcomes before you have the information they require, and not treating your grief, your anger, your ambivalence, or your faith as obstacles to recovery rather than as integral parts of it.

The chapters ahead draw on two streams of knowledge that are rarely held together in a single book: the research literature on betrayal trauma and affair recovery, and the resources of a faith tradition that takes suffering seriously enough to have a vocabulary for it. I hold both because the people who are actually living through this tend to inhabit both and because the best clinical work on betrayal trauma and the deepest resources of the contemplative tradition are, at their cores, saying something similar: that healing from serious harm requires honesty, that it takes longer than you think, and that you are not as alone in it as it currently feels.

* * *

This book is organized in four movements, each corresponding to a phase of the recovery process as the research and my clinical experience describe it.

The first movement — Chapters One through Three — addresses the immediate aftermath of discovery: what happened to you, why it affected you the way it did, and what your mind and body are doing in response. If you are in the early days or weeks after discovery, these chapters are where you are. They are designed to give you language for an experience that often feels beyond language, and to help you understand that your responses, however frightening or disorienting they may feel, are not signs of weakness.

The second movement — Chapters Four through Six — addresses the questions of the middle period: whether the conditions for recovery are present, how to hold the decision about your future without being destroyed by the pressure to resolve it prematurely, and how to understand the affair in ways that make it legible without asking you to excuse it. Understanding what happened is not the same as forgiving it. It is a different and more primary task: building a map of a terrain you need to navigate.

The third movement — Chapters Seven through Nine — follows the Gottman Institute's research-based model of affair recovery through its three phases: Atonement, Attunement, and Attachment. These chapters are addressed primarily to the betrayed spouse working to evaluate whether real repair is occurring but they are also useful for understanding what repair requires, regardless of whether your partner is currently providing it.

The fourth movement — Chapters Ten and Eleven — addresses what the previous movements often overlook: what persists after the acute phase has passed, what living forward actually involves, and what kind of person is being made from what has happened. Recovery is not an erasure. It is a reorganization. These chapters take the long view.

* * *

Throughout the book, you will follow the stories of two composite figures whose experiences together represent the range of betrayal trauma. Claire is a betrayed wife in her late thirties navigating the aftermath of her husband Daniel's affair, a path that eventually leads toward a rebuilt marriage. Evan is a betrayed husband in his late forties whose wife Amber's sustained infidelity, and her unwillingness to offer honest accountability, leads him on a different path. Both stories are drawn from the composite experience of real clients and research participants. Neither is a single person, though both feel like one.

We follow them together because their stories need to be held together. Recovery from betrayal is not a single journey. It is many journeys through the same impossible terrain, with different equipment, different traveling companions, and different destinations. The chapters ahead try to honor that complexity without surrendering the clarity that people who are suffering need.

* * *

A word about what this book is not. It is not a book about whether you should stay or leave. Chapter Five addresses that question at length, but the book itself does not have an answer for you. That answer lives in the particulars of your situation, the honesty of your partner, the conditions of your relationship, the children or community or covenant that shapes what is possible and no book can access those particulars the way you can.

It is not a book that requires faith to use. The clinical research I draw on does not require a theological framework, and the chapters that engage faith resources are designed to be useful to readers who locate themselves there without being inaccessible to those who do not.

It is not a book that promises healing by the final chapter. What it promises is something more modest and, we think, more useful: an honest account of what the research shows, what recovery actually looks like, what it requires, and what becomes possible when it is done seriously and with adequate support. That is not a small promise. It is, in my experience, the one that people who are suffering most need kept.

* * *

You are still here. You picked up this book, which means some part of you has not given up on the possibility that things can be different from the way they are right now.

Let's begin.

Part 1: When the Ground Disappears

Chapter One: The Day Everything Changed

"The worst part wasn't finding out. The worst part was realizing I would have to keep living after."
— from a letter never sent

There is a before and an after. You may not have known, in the moment you found out, that you were crossing a permanent threshold. Some people describe the discovery as slow, a creeping suspicion that finally crystallized into undeniable truth. Others describe it as sudden: a text message glimpsed over a shoulder, a receipt that didn't make sense, a confession that arrived without warning while standing in an ordinary kitchen on an ordinary Tuesday. However it happened, the world divided. There was life before this, and now there is life after.

If you are reading these words in the early days or weeks after discovering a partner's affair, you may feel as though the floor has disappeared beneath you. You may be in shock, functional enough to make coffee and answer emails, but operating behind a kind of glass. Or you may be the opposite: flooded, unable to eat or sleep, unable to stop replaying images and questions in a loop that never quite resolves. Both of these responses, and everything in between, make complete sense. They are not signs of weakness or instability. They are the predictable, even necessary, responses of a mind and body that have been profoundly hurt.

This book is written for you. It is written for the person who is not sure they can trust what they are feeling. For the person who keeps asking why and keeps getting answers that don't satisfy. For the person who loves their partner and cannot imagine a future with them, and also cannot imagine a future without them, and is exhausted by holding both of those truths at the same time. For the person who is trying to be strong for their children, their marriage, their faith, their family and who is doing all of that while quietly falling apart.

It is also written for the person who is completely alone in this. Perhaps you have not told anyone. Perhaps you cannot. You may be protecting your spouse's reputation, or your children's sense of stability, or your own pride. You may live in a community where there is no safe person to tell. You may have told one person and felt more alone after than before. Whatever the reason, if you are carrying this without support, I want you to know that you are not invisible here. This book is one place where you do not have to pretend.

* * *

What happened to you was a serious harm. That needs to be said before anything else. That sounds obvious. But many betrayed spouses, in the weeks and months following discovery, find themselves minimizing what occurred, sometimes because their partner minimizes it, sometimes because their community minimizes it, and sometimes because minimizing is its own form of survival. "Other people have it worse," they tell themselves. "At least it wasn't a long-term affair." "At least there were no children involved." "At least it's over now." These comparisons, while understandable, can work against healing. They can cut off access to the grief and anger that are not only legitimate, but necessary.

An affair is not simply a sexual transgression or a failure of impulse control. It is a violation of a covenant, a set of promises that formed the architecture of a shared life. It involves sustained deception, often over months or years. It means that a significant portion of the life you thought you were living was not the life that was actually occurring. The meals, the conversations, the plans, the intimacy, all of it existed inside a context that was not what you believed it to be. That kind of betrayal reaches into the past as well as the present. It doesn't just change what is happening now. It changes how you understand what has already happened.

Researchers who study betrayal trauma, the specific psychological harm that results from being seriously wronged by someone we depend on have documented that this kind of injury produces responses that closely resemble those of post-traumatic stress. Intrusive memories. Hypervigilance. Emotional numbness alternating with overwhelming feeling. Difficulty concentrating. Sleep disruption. Physical symptoms including fatigue, nausea, and a racing heart. These are not signs that you are "going crazy." They are signs that your nervous system is doing exactly what it was built to do when safety has been shattered (Freyd, 1996).

Understanding that your responses are trauma responses matters, because it changes how you relate to yourself during this period. You are not overreacting. You are not too sensitive. You are not weak for being undone by this. You are a person whose trust was broken in a place where trust was meant to be safe, and your mind and body are responding accordingly.

* * *

One of the most important things to understand about why betrayal hurts the way it does is that marriage, or any committed intimate partnership, is an attachment relationship.

Attachment, in the psychological sense, refers to the deep emotional bonds humans form with specific others across the lifespan. These bonds are not optional. They are biological. We are wired, from birth, to seek proximity to a person who feels safe, who will respond to our distress, and who we can count on when things go wrong. In early life, these bonds form between children and caregivers. In adult life, they most often center in a romantic partnership. Our partner becomes, in the language of researcher John Bowlby who first articulated attachment theory, our primary attachment figure: the person we turn to first, and the person whose availability shapes our fundamental sense of security in the world (Bowlby, 1988).

This is not a metaphor. It is a neurobiological reality. When we feel secure in our closest relationship, the brain's threat-detection systems operate at lower levels of activation. We can think more clearly, regulate our emotions more effectively, and engage more openly with the world. The secure base provided by a trusted partner changes how the nervous system functions. Conversely, when that security is disrupted, when the primary attachment figure becomes a source of threat rather than safety, the nervous system responds as though the ground has given way beneath us. Because, in a very real sense, it has.

Sue Johnson, developer of Emotionally Focused Therapy and couples therapist, building on Bowlby's work, has described infidelity as an "attachment injury", a specific kind of wound that occurs when a partner fails to respond, or actively harms, during a moment of acute vulnerability (Johnson, Makinen, & Millikin, 2001). This framing helps explain why betrayal can feel so destabilizing even when the betrayed partner was not aware of the affair while it was happening. The injury is not only about the specific acts of deception. It is about the rupture in the fundamental structure of safety that the relationship was meant to provide. It is about the discovery that the person who was supposed to be the safe harbor was, for a period of time, the source of the storm.

This is why healing from infidelity is not simply a matter of processing hurt feelings and deciding to move on. It requires rebuilding something structural, a sense of safety in the relationship and, often, a sense of safety in oneself and in one's own perceptions. Both of those take time. Both of those require more than good intentions.

* * *

In these early days, you may not be sure what you are feeling, because you may be feeling everything at once. Shock. Grief. Rage. A strange, dissociated numbness. An almost physical longing for the partner you thought you had. Disgust. Confusion. The surreal sensation of watching yourself from the outside. Shame that belongs to someone else but has somehow landed on you. An irrational desire to fix this, to do something, anything, to make the pain stop. And underneath all of it, a question that will not go away: Why?

All of this is normal. Not comfortable, not easy, but normal. The fluctuation between states is one of the most disorienting aspects of the early period. You may feel numb for a day and then be ambushed by grief while making dinner. You may feel certain about what you want and then uncertain about everything twenty-four hours later. You may feel hatred for your partner and love for them in the same hour and feel guilty about both. Trauma researchers sometimes describe this oscillation as characteristic of how the mind processes overwhelming experience: moving between approach and avoidance, between confronting the reality and needing a rest from it (Stroebe & Schut, 1999). The back-and-forth is not a sign that you are confused or unstable. It is the mind doing the slow, difficult work of taking in something it was not prepared to receive.

You may also notice that your body is involved in this in ways that surprise you. Sleep may be impossible, or you may sleep too much and wake feeling no better. Appetite may disappear. You may feel a persistent tightness in your chest or throat. Some people report what can only be described as a physical ache, a grief that is not merely emotional but visceral, located somewhere in the body. This makes neurobiological sense. Social pain and physical pain share overlapping neural pathways. Being rejected or betrayed by a person we love activates some of the same brain regions as physical injury (Eisenberger, 2012). The body takes betrayal seriously. You should take it seriously too.

If you are finding it difficult to eat, sleep, or function at a basic level, please consider reaching out for professional support. A therapist who is trained in trauma and experienced with infidelity recovery can be an important part of your support system during this period. This book can offer understanding and guidance, but it is not a substitute for skilled human presence. We will return to this point throughout, including some guidance on what to look for in a therapist and how to find one if resources are limited.

* * *

This book is not a guarantee. It will not promise that your relationship can be saved, because that depends on more than you, and more than this book, can determine. It will not promise that your pain will end by a certain chapter or a certain month. Healing from betrayal trauma is not linear, and anyone who tells you otherwise is not telling the full truth.

What this book will do is walk alongside you. It will try to help you understand what is happening inside you, psychologically, physically, relationally, and spiritually so that you can make sense of your own experience. It will try to help you think clearly about your situation, even when clarity is hard to come by. It will offer some guidance on what healthy repair looks like, so that you can recognize it or recognize its absence. And it will try, throughout, to treat you as an intelligent adult who deserves honest information rather than false comfort.

I will not assume your partner has ended the affair. I will not assume you have been given the truth. I will not assume your partner is in therapy, is remorseful, or is showing real willingness to repair. Some readers will be in relationships where all of those things are true, and those readers face a different set of challenges than readers who are still in the dark, or still being deceived, or still waiting to find out whether their partner is willing to be honest at all. I will try to speak to all of these situations.

This book also does not assume that staying in your relationship is the right choice, or that leaving is the right choice. Both staying and leaving can be wise, depending on what is actually present in your specific situation. What we care about here is not the preservation of the institution at any cost. What we care about is your safety, your dignity, and your real wellbeing and your ability to make decisions about your own life that are grounded in reality rather than in fear, shame, or pressure.

For readers who hold faith commitments: this book takes those commitments seriously. Covenant, forgiveness, grace, repentance, and redemption are not foreign concepts here. But they will not be used to rush you past your pain, to silence your anger, to pressure you toward reconciliation before safety has been established, or to shame you for having limits.

There is a pattern that appears frequently in faith communities in the wake of suffering and in the face of betrayal specifically that needs to be named directly. Psychotherapist John Welwood (1984) coined the term *spiritual bypass* in 1984 to describe the tendency to use spiritual beliefs and practices to sidestep rather than engage with unresolved pain and emotional wounds. In Christian contexts, spiritual bypass often sounds like this: *just pray about it; everything happens for a reason; choose joy; forgive and move on.* These responses are not always offered without care. But when they are used to silence grief, suppress anger, or move a wounded person toward a resolution they are not yet ready for, they function as a detour around the very pain that healing requires moving through. In *Finding Hope in the Ashes: Lament, Healing, and the God Who Stays* (Tanner, 2025), the practice of biblical lament is explored as the faithful alternative to spiritual bypass not the absence of faith, but its most honest expression when life is at its hardest. That framework shapes this book as well. Faith, at its best, holds truth and mercy together. I will try to do the same.

* * *

Somewhere ahead of you, not immediately, and not easily, there is ground that is more stable than where you are standing right now. That is not a promise of restored marriage. It is not a promise of painless days. It is a promise that the disorientation you are feeling in this early period is not your permanent address. People do survive this. Many of them, with time, real repair work, and honest support, find that they have rebuilt something, whether inside their marriage or outside of it, that is more clear-eyed, more honest, and in some ways more solid than what existed before. Not because the betrayal was worth it. Never that. But because the human capacity for meaning-making and resilience is real, and because healing, though hard, is truly possible.

The research on post-traumatic growth, the phenomenon in which people who have survived significant suffering report new strengths, deepened relationships, and greater clarity about what matters does not suggest that trauma is secretly a gift. It suggests that the human spirit, given sufficient support and time, can find its footing even after profound loss (Tedeschi & Calhoun, 2004). I hold that finding carefully here: without minimizing the harm, and without rushing toward silver linings. But I hold it, because you deserve to know that the research supports what many survivors have found to be true in their own experience.

For now, though, you do not have to know any of that yet. You do not have to be hopeful. You do not have to be strong. You do not have to know what you want or what comes next. You only have to keep reading.

Looking Ahead

What happened to you on the day of discovery set something in motion. The chapters immediately ahead are about what that something looks like from the inside: the specific ways betrayal trauma registers in the mind, the body, and the attachment system in the weeks and months that follow. Chapter Two maps that interior landscape, the intrusive thoughts that arrive without warning, the hypervigilance that makes rest impossible, the grief that comes in waves and the numbness that comes between them. Understanding what is happening to you, and why, is not a substitute for the recovery work ahead. But it is the beginning of it. You cannot navigate terrain you cannot name.

References

Bowlby, J. (1988). *A secure base: Parent-child attachment and healthy human development.* Basic Books.

Eisenberger, N. I. (2012). The pain of social disconnection: Examining the shared neural underpinnings of physical and social pain. *Nature Reviews Neuroscience*, 13(6), 421–434. https://doi.org/10.1038/nrn3231

Freyd, J. J. (1996). *Betrayal trauma: The logic of forgetting childhood abuse.* Harvard University Press.

Johnson, S. M., Makinen, J. A., & Millikin, J. W. (2001). Attachment injuries in couple relationships: A new perspective on impasses in couples therapy. *Journal of Marital and Family Therapy*, 27(2), 145–155. https://doi.org/10.1111/j.1752-0606.2001.tb01152.x

Stroebe, M., & Schut, H. (1999). The dual process model of coping with bereavement: Rationale and description. *Death Studies*, 23(3), 197–224. https://doi.org/10.1080/074811899201046

Tanner, M. N. (2025). *Finding hope in the ashes: Lament, healing, and the God who stays.* HealingChoice Publishing.

Tedeschi, R. G., & Calhoun, L. G. (2004). Posttraumatic growth: Conceptual foundations and empirical evidence. *Psychological Inquiry*, 15(1), 1–18. https://doi.org/10.1207/s15327965pli1501_01

Welwood, J. (1984). Principles of inner work: Psychological and spiritual. *Journal of Transpersonal Psychology*, 16(1), 63–73.

Chapter Two: When the Ground Disappears

"The body keeps the score."
— Bessel van der Kolk, The Body Keeps the Score (2014)

Claire

Claire sat in the parking lot of her office for twenty-three minutes before she could make herself go inside. She had been doing this for eleven days. The drive to work was fine. The parking lot was manageable. It was the walk through the lobby, past the receptionist who would smile at her, that stopped her. Because the receptionist did not know. Her colleagues did not know. The man in the corner office who had coached her through a difficult performance review did not know. They all moved through the building as though nothing had changed, and in their world, nothing had. In hers, everything had.

This is where we find Claire, and it is where many readers find themselves as well: in the strange, disorienting space between a world that has shattered and a world that has not yet registered what happened. The external life continues. The internal life is barely recognizable.

This chapter is about what is happening inside that internal life. Not in general terms, but concretely: what trauma does to the nervous system, what betrayal does to the attachment bond, and why the responses that feel so extreme and so uncontrollable are, in fact, neither extreme nor irrational. They are the predictable, well-documented consequences of a particular kind of wound.

Understanding that wound does not make it hurt less. But it may make it feel less like evidence of something wrong with you and more like evidence that you are a human being whose nervous system is working exactly as it was designed to.

Betrayal Is Not Simply a Relationship Problem

Most people, before they experience it, imagine that learning of a partner's affair would feel like grief. Painful, yes. Disorienting, perhaps. But recognizable. Something in the emotional vocabulary they already possess. What they find instead is something that does not fit the vocabulary they have.

The difference matters, and it is not merely semantic. Grief and trauma behave differently. Grief is anchored in the past: something has been lost, and the work of mourning is to integrate that loss over time. Trauma is not anchored in the past. It lives in the present tense. The nervous system, registering that something dangerous occurred, remains activated and alert, scanning for a threat that still feels nearby.

Betrayal trauma combines both. There is real loss: the marriage as it was understood, the future that was assumed, the partner as the betrayed spouse believed they knew them. There is also something that functions like a survival response, the immune system of the psyche activating to protect against further harm. When these arrive together, the result is an experience that most people struggle to describe and almost no one adequately prepares for.

Jennifer Freyd, a research psychologist at the University of Oregon, coined the term betrayal trauma in the early 1990s to describe the distinctive psychological injury that occurs when someone who is deeply depended upon violates the trust of the relationship (Freyd, 1994). Freyd's original framework focused on childhood abuse, but subsequent research has extended it to adult intimate partnerships. Her central insight was that betrayal by a close attachment figure carries a qualitatively different weight than betrayal by a stranger or acquaintance. The relationship was more important, certainly. But the deeper wound lies in the fact that the very person who functioned as a source of safety has become, instead, a source of threat. The system is thrown into a contradiction it was not built to resolve.

Research drawing on clinical samples of betrayed partners has consistently found that a substantial proportion present with intrusive symptoms, hyperarousal, and avoidance patterns that meet most diagnostic criteria for post-traumatic stress disorder and are clinically indistinguishable from those seen in survivors of other recognized traumas (Gordon, Baucom, & Snyder, 2004). This is not a rhetorical point. It is a finding with direct clinical and personal implications: if what you are experiencing resembles what trauma survivors experience, it is because it is what trauma survivors experience.

What the Affair Actually Did to the Relationship

Before we can understand what the betrayed partner is living through, we need to understand something about what an affair does inside a marriage, not just to it.

Shirley Glass, a psychologist who spent more than thirty years studying infidelity, described affairs as involving a fundamental reorganization of emotional and physical boundaries (Glass, 2003). In a healthy marriage, the couple maintains what Glass called a wall and a window: openness toward each other and appropriate boundaries with outsiders. Affairs reverse this structure. The unfaithful partner builds a wall of secrecy against the spouse and opens a window of intimacy toward the affair partner. The marriage, from the outside, may appear unchanged. From the inside, its architecture has been quietly inverted.

Glass documented something that betrayed partners often describe but struggle to name: the sense that the marriage they thought they were living in was not the marriage that actually existed. The conversations, the vacations, the ordinary Tuesday evenings, all of it was happening alongside something the betrayed partner did not know about and had no way of knowing about. Their understanding of their own life was, in a precise and verifiable sense, wrong.

This is part of what makes betrayal so disorienting. It is not merely that something bad happened. It is that something bad was happening, possibly for months or years, while the betrayed partner was operating on entirely false information. Their memories now require reexamination. Their sense of their own perceptiveness has been called into question. Even their trust in their own experience becomes uncertain.

John Gottman's research on trust offers a precise framework for understanding what has been damaged. Gottman describes trust as built through thousands of small moments of attunement, responsiveness, and reliability over time. Each moment of real connection is what he calls a trust deposit. Each moment of dismissal, deception, or turning away is a withdrawal. Trust, in this model, is not a single decision or feeling but an accumulated relational structure, something built slowly and damaged quickly (Gottman & Silver, 1999).

The discovery of an affair is not simply a large withdrawal from that account. It retroactively calls into question the validity of the deposits. If this person was capable of sustained deception, what else may have been performance rather than presence? The betrayed partner is not being paranoid when they ask this question. They are responding accurately to information that makes the question reasonable.

The Attachment Bond Under Siege

To understand why betrayal produces responses of this intensity, it helps to understand what the attachment bond is and what it does in adult intimate relationships.

Attachment theory, developed by the British psychiatrist John Bowlby and extended by decades of subsequent research, describes the deep biological system that governs our bonds with significant others across the lifespan (Bowlby, 1969, 1973, 1980). Bowlby argued that human beings are not simply social animals who prefer company. We are attachment animals: we are wired to seek proximity to specific others, to use those people as a secure base from which to engage the world, and to experience their unavailability as a real threat to wellbeing.

In adult romantic partnerships, this system does not disappear. It transforms, transferring its primary orientation from early caregivers to intimate partners. We turn to our partners when we are sick, frightened, or uncertain. We organize considerable portions of our lives around maintaining proximity and connection with them. When they are reliably available, we feel safer in the world. When they are not, we feel the absence as something closer to threat than inconvenience.

This is why intimate betrayal carries such weight. Someone we love has done something hurtful. But the deeper wound is that the person who functioned as our secure base has proven to be the source of the threat. The attachment system, organized around this person as safety, must now process the fact that this person was actively deceptive, pursuing their own desires at the expense of the relationship, and concealing this systematically. The safe harbor was not what it appeared to be.

Sue Johnson, whose Emotionally Focused Therapy draws directly on attachment science, has described affairs as attachment injuries: moments of abandonment or betrayal at a time of perceived need so severe that they continue to disrupt the relational bond long after the original event (Johnson et al., 2001). The term is precise. An attachment injury is not a bad memory. It is a structural rupture in the emotional architecture of the relationship. Until it is adequately addressed, it functions as a fault line beneath every subsequent interaction, capable of reopening without warning.

For the betrayed partner, this means something important: the reason you cannot simply decide to move on, the reason conversations about ordinary things still feel unsafe, the reason your partner's reassurances do not yet register as real, is not that you are being stubborn or punishing. It is that your attachment system is accurately registering that the bond it depended on was broken, and it requires evidence, not promises, before it can begin to reorganize around a new sense of safety.

What Happens in the Brain and Body

The experience of betrayal is not metaphorical. It is physiological. When betrayal is discovered, the brain's threat detection system, centered in the amygdala, responds the way it responds to any credible danger: by triggering the stress response. Adrenaline and cortisol flood the system. Heart rate increases. Respiration changes. The muscles prepare for action. The prefrontal cortex, the region responsible for rational deliberation, language, and measured judgment, is partially taken offline in favor of systems designed for speed and survival.

Those first moments, hours, and sometimes days after discovery can feel fragmented and surreal. People report trouble forming sentences. They find themselves unable to perform simple tasks. They feel simultaneously hyper-alert and strangely disconnected from their own bodies. Some describe an out-of-body quality to the experience. Others describe a narrowing of vision, a roaring in the ears, or the sensation that the room has shifted in some way they cannot name.

These are not signs of weakness. They are signs that the nervous system registered something it categorized as dangerous and activated accordingly. Neuroscientist Naomi Eisenberger's research at UCLA demonstrated that social pain, including the pain of rejection and relational rupture, activates many of the same neural regions as physical pain (Eisenberger & Lieberman, 2004). The body does not distinguish cleanly between a broken bone and a broken bond. Both register as threat. Both produce a survival response.

What follows in the days and weeks after discovery is what trauma researchers describe as a biphasic response: oscillation between states of hyperarousal and states of numbing or shutdown (Herman, 1992). Betrayed partners often describe this cycle with confusion. One moment they are consumed by overwhelming emotion: rage, grief, panic, an unbearable need to know more. The next moment they feel strangely flat, detached, unable to feel anything at all. Then the intensity returns.

Judith Herman's foundational work on trauma describes these alternating states as intrusion and constriction. Intrusion includes flashbacks, intrusive thoughts, nightmares, and hypervigilance. Constriction includes emotional numbing, withdrawal, difficulty concentrating, and a sense of unreality. Each is uncomfortable. Each serves a psychological function. Intrusion keeps the mind reviewing the threat, trying to make sense of it. Constriction provides a temporary reduction of unbearable intensity. Neither is something the betrayed partner is choosing. Both are the nervous system attempting to cope with information too large to integrate at once.

Bessel van der Kolk's work on traumatic memory adds another dimension. The brain encodes traumatic experience differently than ordinary experience. Rather than forming coherent narrative memories with clear sequence and context, traumatic memories tend to be stored in fragments: sensory impressions, images, and body sensations that do not carry the markers of pastness that ordinary memories carry (van der Kolk, 2014). When these memories are activated by a trigger, a question, a tone of voice, a particular time of day, they return not as something remembered but as something experienced again, right now.

The question a betrayed partner asks at two in the morning is not always a rational request for information. Sometimes it is the trauma reactivating, the mind and body trying once more to make the incomprehensible comprehensible. That same image returns despite every effort of will. The mind is not malfunctioning. It is trying to process something it cannot yet absorb.

* * *

Evan

Evan had been married for twenty-two years when he found the messages. His wife, Amber, had not had a brief emotional connection. She had been involved with a coworker for three years. Three years of dinners he thought were work events. Three years of a marriage that, from where he stood, had looked solid. He had not been suspicious. He had had no reason to be.

What Evan experienced after discovery looked different from Claire's in some ways. He did not cry much. He did not have difficulty speaking. He went to work the following Monday, sat in meetings, answered emails, and by all external appearances was functioning normally. But he was not sleeping. He was replaying conversations going back years, re-examining the timeline of his marriage with the obsessive attention of someone trying to locate exactly where the ground had given way beneath them. He felt, he said, like a detective investigating a crime in which he was both the investigator and the evidence.

His response and Claire's look different on the surface. Underneath, they are expressions of the same wound. The body and mind, facing something they cannot yet integrate, find different paths through the same impossible terrain.

***

Why You Cannot Think Your Way Through This

One of the cruelest aspects of betrayal trauma is that it tends to be invisible to everyone around the betrayed partner, and sometimes to the betrayed partner themselves. There are rarely visible wounds. The person may look functional while internally experiencing something that has more in common with the aftermath of a serious accident than an ordinary relationship difficulty.

This invisibility generates pressure, both internal and external, to regulate more quickly than is possible. Partners, family members, well-meaning friends, and sometimes therapists unfamiliar with betrayal trauma may encourage the betrayed partner to calm down, to stop bringing it up, to take the long view, to focus on forgiveness. The betrayed partner, often already humiliated by what has happened, may internalize these messages and begin to pathologize their own responses. Am I losing my mind? Why can't I get past this? What is wrong with me?

The answer to that last question is: nothing. The experience of being unable to simply move on is not a sign of weakness or inflexibility. It is a sign that the nervous system is doing exactly what it was designed to do when something threatening has occurred.

Rationality returns as the nervous system regulates. This process takes time and it cannot be rushed by willpower alone. It can be supported: by physical safety, by accurate information, by consistent and trustworthy behavior over time, by good therapeutic help. But the timeline is not under conscious control and cannot be demanded into submission. Anyone who tells you otherwise is asking you to override a biological process with an act of will. That is not a reasonable request.

The Particular Problem of Not Knowing

That difficulty processing becomes acute when the threat itself remains unclear. If you have not received full and honest disclosure from your partner, what you are navigating is compounded in its own way that deserves direct acknowledgment.

Ambiguity amplifies the threat response. When a threat is known and concrete, the brain can orient to it. When the threat is uncertain, when there may be more to learn, when the account has changed, when your instincts are telling you something does not add up, the threat detection system remains perpetually activated. It cannot downshift because it does not know what it is dealing with.

Paul Peluso's clinical work on disclosure and infidelity recovery is relevant here. Peluso (2007) argued that the manner and completeness of disclosure is not a secondary concern in affair recovery but a foundational one. Premature closure, meaning pressure to move forward before an honest account has been established, tends to produce what he calls false recovery: a surface-level resumption of normal life that rests on an unstable foundation and is likely to collapse when the fuller truth eventually emerges, as it usually does.

Partial disclosure is not a kindness. The nervous system experiences it as ongoing exposure to threat. If your partner has told you some things but you sense there is more, or if the story has changed more than once, or if your instincts are registering inconsistency, your hypervigilance is not irrational. It is an appropriate response to an environment that has not yet proven safe.

Genuine repair requires honest foundation. This book will address disclosure in depth in a later chapter. For now, you cannot heal from something that is still ongoing, and you cannot build on ground that has not been cleared. If you are still in uncertainty, your nervous system is not overreacting. It is responding accurately to a situation that has not yet been made safe.

Hypervigilance Is Not Paranoia

One of the most disorienting experiences for betrayed partners is the sudden onset of hypervigilance: an exhausting, involuntary state of heightened alertness in which the mind perpetually scans the environment for signs of danger. You notice when your partner is five minutes late. You study the tone of their voice when they answer a simple question. You track their eyes. You analyze their phone habits. You examine their explanations for internal consistency.

From the outside, this can look like jealousy or the desire to control. From the inside, it feels compulsive and depleting, like something you cannot turn off even when you want to. And you probably do want to turn it off. Living in this state costs enormous energy and poisons ordinary moments.

But hypervigilance is not jealousy and it is not paranoia. It is the brain doing precisely what it evolved to do after a threat: scanning the environment for signs that the threat might recur. The same mental apparatus that helped our ancestors survive in physically dangerous environments is now oriented toward detecting relational deception. It cannot easily distinguish between an actual new threat and a pattern that merely resembles one. It simply keeps scanning.

There is something else worth naming here. Many betrayed partners report that they had a sense something was wrong before they knew. They noticed something, felt something, registered something their partner dismissed or explained away. Qualitative research on the discovery process documents that this is common: the discovery event is often preceded by a period of vague unease that partners found themselves talked or reasoned out of trusting (Mitchell et al., 2025).

The hypervigilance that emerges after discovery is the same sensitivity that was already present, now fully activated and no longer deniable. This does not mean that every fear will prove accurate going forward. Healing involves, gradually, the nervous system learning through accumulated evidence that the environment has become safer. But that learning cannot be demanded. It happens through consistency, honesty, and time, not through being told to calm down.

Intrusive Thoughts and the Images That Will Not Leave

Perhaps nothing distresses betrayed partners more than the intrusive thoughts and images that arrive without invitation and resist dismissal. The mind generates scenes it cannot confirm. It produces images of the affair partner. It rehearses possible encounters. It asks the same questions on an endless loop. Why? What did they have that I don't? Did you love them? What were you thinking when you were with me?

These thoughts are not a choice. If they were, everyone would choose to stop having them. They are a form of intrusive re-experiencing, the trauma demanding to be processed and understood, even at three in the morning, even in the middle of an ordinary conversation.

Daniel Wegner's research on thought suppression is relevant here. Wegner demonstrated that actively trying not to think about something often increases its frequency, the well-known white bear effect (Wegner et al., 1987). The mind, checking to confirm it is successfully suppressing the unwanted thought, inevitably returns that thought to attention. This is a cruel irony for someone who desperately wants to stop thinking about the affair. The effort of suppression can make it worse.

Fife and colleagues (2008), in their research on the recovery experiences of betrayed partners, found that intrusive thoughts and images were among the most universally reported and most distressing features of the post-discovery period. What was notable in their findings was not simply the presence of these thoughts but the shame that accompanied them: betrayed partners often felt that having such thoughts was itself evidence of something wrong with them, rather than a predictable feature of the trauma they were processing.

That shame is misplaced. The images and questions will not stop when you want them to. They will diminish as the trauma processes. The rate at which that happens depends on many things: whether the threat has truly ended, whether honest information is available, whether the nervous system has the safety and support it needs to gradually integrate what has happened. What does not help, over time, is suppression, shame about having the thoughts, or the belief that their presence means something is fundamentally wrong with you.

Grief Without a Clean Object

Betrayal produces grief, but grief of an unusual kind. In ordinary bereavement, the loss is clear. In betrayal, it is not. The marriage may still exist. The partner is still physically present. But something has died that resists easy naming.

What exactly are you grieving? The past you believed you had, which may or may not have been real. The future you assumed was waiting, now destabilized. The version of your partner you thought you knew and the version of yourself who trusted them. The safety you believed existed in your home, your bed, your life. Some people grieve a quality of ease, the openness with which they once moved through their days, that they are not sure they can recover.

There are also secondary losses: the memories that must now be reexamined, the photographs that carry different associations, the places that are now freighted with new meaning, the ordinary pleasures that are now tainted by what was happening alongside them. Fife and colleagues found that betrayed partners consistently described this dimensionality of loss as something they had not anticipated and that others around them consistently failed to understand (Fife et al., 2008). Friends offered comfort appropriate to simpler losses. The complexity went unwitnessed.

Stroebe and Schut's dual process model of grief is useful here. They propose that healthy grieving involves oscillation between loss-orientation, actively confronting and processing the loss, and restoration-orientation, attending to life tasks and secondary consequences (Stroebe & Schut, 1999). The betrayed partner must do both, often simultaneously, often without adequate support. They must grieve what has been lost while also making decisions, managing daily life, possibly parenting, and trying to assess whether the marriage has any viable future.

This is an enormous amount to carry. The grief does not move in orderly stages. It spirals. It revisits. A date on the calendar, a song, an off-hand remark can reopen it completely. This is not evidence that you are failing to heal. It is evidence that you are grieving something real and complex, and that complex grief takes time.

Shame That Does Not Belong to You

One of the most painful and least discussed dimensions of betrayal is the shame that betrayed partners frequently carry, a shame that does not belong to them but that attaches to them anyway.

Shame, in its essence, is the feeling that something is fundamentally wrong with me, not merely with something I have done. It is distinct from guilt, which says I did something bad. Shame says I am something bad. The betrayed partner did not act wrongly, yet shame is often more present in them than in the partner who did.

Why? Several dynamics converge. There is social shame: what will others think of me, of my family, of my marriage. There is the shame of imagined comparison: the belief that the affair partner must have been more attractive, more interesting, more something. There is the shame of having been deceived: of having been, as some people describe it, a fool in their own home. And there is a shame that attaches to the body, to the sexual dimensions of betrayal, to the knowledge that one's partner was intimate with someone else while also intimate with them.

This shame is not rational, but it is very common, and it is not yours to carry. Betrayal is not caused by the betrayed partner's inadequacy. People are not unfaithful because their spouses are insufficient. They are unfaithful because something within themselves, their character, their avoidance, their choices, their unaddressed unhappiness, drew them in a direction they did not resist. That is a reflection on them, not on you.

This is not the same as saying your marriage was without difficulty or that there was nothing to address. Most marriages have areas that need growth. But the decision to handle relational dissatisfaction through deception and infidelity was the unfaithful partner's choice, made by them, belonging to them. Whatever your contributions to the state of the marriage, you did not cause the affair. Its discovery is not a verdict on your worth.

Recognizing where the shame comes from does not make it disappear immediately. But it may allow you to hold it with slightly less certainty, to examine it rather than simply inhabit it. That examination is part of healing.

Ambivalence Is Not Weakness

If you feel conflicting things simultaneously, love and rage, a desire to stay and a desire to leave, moments of compassion for your partner and moments of wishing they did not exist, you are not unstable. You are in a situation that calls for conflicting responses.

Ambivalence in the wake of betrayal is nearly universal, and it is poorly understood by most people outside the experience. Friends and family, wanting to be helpful, often push toward resolution. Leave. Or: Give them another chance. Or: You need to decide. What they are usually expressing is their own discomfort with ambiguity rather than wisdom about your situation. Ambivalence is uncomfortable to witness.

But the middle is exactly where many betrayed partners are for a sustained period, and that middle is legitimate. A marriage of any real depth is not something that can be quickly evaluated and sorted. The person who wronged you profoundly may also be a person you know in complicated ways that an outside observer cannot fully appreciate. The choice between staying and leaving may be deeply unclear, and it may remain unclear for longer than anyone around you is comfortable with.

Fife and colleagues found that ambivalence in betrayed partners was not only common but often prolonged; others frequently misread it as indecision or weakness, and external pressure to resolve it prematurely was itself a barrier to genuine healing (Fife et al., 2008). The pressure to choose quickly, in either direction, rarely serves the betrayed partner.

This book will not tell you what to do. It will try to help you develop the clarity, stability, and accurate information you need to make the decisions that are yours to make. Staying after betrayal is sometimes wise and sometimes not. Leaving is sometimes wise and sometimes not. The determining factors are not simple, and they are unlikely to be clear in the immediate aftermath of discovery. Decisions made in the acute phase of trauma, when the nervous system is flooded and information is incomplete, are rarely the wisest decisions. There is usually some time. Not unlimited time, but enough to allow the nervous system to settle, information to emerge, and greater clarity to develop.

You Are Not Alone, Even If It Feels That Way

Some readers are carrying this in silence. You have not told anyone. Perhaps you are protecting your partner, your children, or your own sense of dignity. Perhaps you do not have people in your life you trust with something this raw. Perhaps your faith community is the last place you could imagine bringing this, because you already know how it would be received, or you fear what it would cost. Perhaps you tried to tell someone and received a response that left you more alone than before.

The silence of betrayal is its own burden. Trauma that cannot be witnessed and spoken tends to remain locked in the body longer, finding fewer opportunities to be processed and integrated. The research on social support and trauma recovery consistently demonstrates that access to at least one trustworthy witness, someone who can hear your experience without judgment, without agenda, without needing you to resolve it quickly, is among the most important factors in how people move through difficulty (Pennebaker & Smyth, 2016).

This does not mean you must tell anyone right now, or that you must tell everyone. It means that, at some point, finding even one safe person, a good therapist, a trusted friend, a pastor or spiritual director with real wisdom and discretion, a support group with appropriate confidentiality, is likely to be important. Healing was not designed to happen in complete isolation. You were made for connection, and what happened to you wounded you in the exact place where connection lives.

If you have not yet found that person or place, it does not mean you are beyond help. It means you are carrying something heavy without adequate support, and that you deserve better than what you currently have access to. That is worth looking for. You did not deserve what happened to you, and you deserve better than carrying it entirely alone.

* * *

Claire eventually went inside the building. Evan eventually slept. Not because the pain was gone, but because the nervous system, given even a small measure of safety, gradually finds its way toward something sustainable.

What happened to you was not ordinary difficulty. It was a rupture at one of the most core levels of human experience: the bond of trust between intimate partners, the sense of safety within one's own home and one's own life. The responses you are having are not signs of fragility. They are evidence that something serious happened, that you are a person with an intact nervous system, and that your mind and body are doing the difficult work of trying to make sense of something that resists easy sense.

The chapters ahead will try to offer what this one has worked toward: a clear map of the territory you are crossing, the knowledge that others have crossed it before you, and the evidence, drawn from research and from the accumulated experience of people who have walked this path, that the other side of it, though different from what you imagined, is reachable.

That is where we are going. We are not there yet. But we are on the way.

Looking Ahead

The chapter ahead shifts the frame from the mind to the body. What Chapter Two has described in psychological terms, the intrusion, the flooding, the hypervigilance, the grief that does not behave like ordinary grief, Chapter Three addresses in physiological ones. Your nervous system has been doing something specific since the day of discovery, and understanding what it is doing, and why it cannot simply be argued out of it, is one of the most important things you can do for yourself in this period. The body is not overreacting. It is responding exactly as it was built to respond. What that means, and what it requires of you, is where we turn next.

References

Bowlby, J. (1969). *Attachment and loss: Vol. 1*. Attachment. Basic Books.

Bowlby, J. (1973). *Attachment and loss: Vol. 2*. Separation: Anxiety and anger. Basic Books.

Bowlby, J. (1980). *Attachment and loss: Vol. 3.* Loss: Sadness and depression. Basic Books.

Gordon, K. C., Baucom, D. H., & Snyder, D. K. (2004). An integrative intervention for promoting recovery from extramarital affairs. *Journal of Marital and Family Therapy*, 30(2), 213–231. https://doi.org/10.1111/j.1752-0606.2004.tb01235.x

Eisenberger, N. I., & Lieberman, M. D. (2004). Why rejection hurts: A common neural alarm system for physical and social pain. *Trends in Cognitive Sciences*, 8(7), 294–300.

Fife, S. T., Weeks, G. R., & Gambescia, N. (2008). Treating infidelity: An integrative approach to resolving trauma and promoting forgiveness. *The Family Journal*, 16(4), 316–322.

Freyd, J. J. (1994). Betrayal trauma: Traumatic amnesia as an adaptive response to childhood abuse. *Ethics & Behavior*, 4(4), 307–329.

Glass, S. P. (2003). *Not "just friends": Rebuilding trust and recovering your sanity after infidelity.* Free Press.

Gottman, J. M., & Silver, N. (1999). *The seven principles for making marriage work.* Crown.

Herman, J. L. (1992). *Trauma and recovery: The aftermath of violence — from domestic abuse to political terror.* Basic Books.

Johnson, S. M., Makinen, J. A., & Millikin, J. W. (2001). Attachment injuries in couple relationships: A new perspective on impasses in couples therapy. *Journal of Marital and Family Therapy*, 27(2), 145–155.

Mitchell, E. A., Brown, K. S., Spencer, J., & Harris, K. (2025). Staying together after infidelity: An exploration of the decision-making process of recovery from the perspective of the injured partner. *Journal of Marital and Family Therapy*, 52(1), 1–12. https://doi.org/10.1111/jmft.70110

Peluso, P. R. (Ed.). (2007). *Infidelity: A practitioner's guide to working with couples in crisis.* Routledge.

Pennebaker, J. W., & Smyth, J. M. (2016). *Opening up by writing it down: How expressive writing improves health and eases emotional pain* (3rd ed.). Guilford Press.

Stroebe, M., & Schut, H. (1999). The dual process model of coping with bereavement: Rationale and description. *Death Studies*, 23(3), 197–224.

van der Kolk, B. A. (2014). *The body keeps the score: Brain, mind, and body in the healing of trauma*. Viking.

Wegner, D. M., Schneider, D. J., Carter, S. R., & White, T. L. (1987). Paradoxical effects of thought suppression. *Journal of Personality and Social Psychology*, 53(1), 5–13.

Chapter Three: What Your Body Already Knows

Claire

Claire did not expect to feel it in her hands. She had called her sister the morning after she found the messages on her husband's phone, and she remembers standing in the kitchen, speaking in what she later described as a very calm voice, telling her sister what she had discovered. Her sister, a nurse, asked if she had eaten. Claire said she didn't think so. Her sister said she sounded odd and asked whether Claire was shaking. Claire looked down at her hands. She was. She had not noticed.

Three weeks later, Claire was waking at 2 a.m. most nights. She had lost eight pounds without trying. She startled badly at sounds she would have ignored before, the refrigerator compressor, a car door outside. At work she was functioning, technically, but she described her concentration as having holes in it. She would read the same paragraph four times and understand nothing. She was exhausted in a way that sleep didn't fix. And she was experiencing a symptom she found frightening and strange: at random moments, an image of her husband would appear in her mind, a particular expression she had seen on his face, or a phrase she had found in a text, and it would arrive with the same force and physicality as a blow. Her heart rate would spike. Her breathing would change. For a few seconds she could think of nothing else. She asked her doctor if something was wrong with her neurologically.

Nothing was wrong with her neurologically. Something had been done to her relationally. That distinction matters, and it is the territory we need to map in this chapter.

The Nervous System Does Not Know It Is Safe

The human nervous system is a threat-detection system. It evolved to do one thing above all else: keep you alive. It scans your environment constantly, below the level of consciousness, for signs of danger. When it detects a threat, it mobilizes the body to respond, flooding the bloodstream with stress hormones, redirecting blood flow to large muscle groups, sharpening certain perceptions while narrowing others. This response is not a personality flaw. It is not weakness. It is one of the most sophisticated survival systems in the biological world.

The problem, for the person who has discovered a partner's betrayal, is that this system cannot distinguish between a physical threat and a relational one. The nervous system does not recognize a category labeled emotional pain and file it separately from physical danger. What it recognizes is threat. And intimate betrayal registers as a profound threat, one that activates the body's alarm system with a force that surprises most people.

Naomi Eisenberger and Matthew Lieberman at UCLA have conducted a series of studies demonstrating that social pain, the pain of rejection, exclusion, and relational loss, activates the same neural regions as physical pain (Eisenberger & Lieberman, 2004; Eisenberger et al., 2003). The dorsal anterior cingulate cortex, a region long associated with the unpleasantness of physical pain, responds to social exclusion with measurable activation. The brain, quite literally, treats being rejected or betrayed the way it treats being hurt. When you describe betrayal as pain, you are not exaggerating. You are being anatomically accurate.

The Stress Cascade

When the threat signal fires, the body's hypothalamic-pituitary-adrenal axis, commonly called the HPA axis, activates a cascade of hormonal responses. The hypothalamus signals the pituitary gland, the pituitary signals the adrenal glands, and cortisol is released into the bloodstream (McEwen, 2007). Cortisol is a stress hormone with a wide range of effects. In short bursts it is useful: it mobilizes energy, sharpens immediate attention, and suppresses immune function that isn't needed in a crisis. In the acute phase of betrayal discovery, many people describe a strange, driven clarity, a kind of activated state in which they are searching for information, replaying events, and functioning on adrenaline. The cortisol response helps explain that experience.

The difficulty comes when the threat does not resolve. If you discover a partner's affair and the situation remains uncertain, with ongoing deception, unclear information, or an ambiguous future, the HPA axis does not receive a clear all-clear signal. Cortisol continues to be released at elevated levels. Chronic cortisol elevation is associated with sleep disruption, appetite changes, immune suppression, impaired memory consolidation, difficulty concentrating, and a general sense of depletion that is physiological in origin (Sapolsky, 2004). When you cannot sleep, cannot eat, cannot concentrate, or feel physically exhausted after weeks of emotional hyperactivation, you are not falling apart. You are experiencing the documented effects of a stress response that has not been given a pathway to resolution.

Cortisol also reshapes thinking itself. Research on stress and executive function consistently shows that chronic stress impairs the prefrontal cortex, the region responsible for planning, decision-making, impulse regulation, and the ability to hold competing possibilities in mind simultaneously (Arnsten, 2009). This means that at precisely the moment when betrayed partners are being asked, by spouses, by family members, and sometimes by well-meaning but poorly timed therapists, to make major decisions about their marriages, their neurological capacity for exactly that kind of reasoning has been compromised. Not eliminated, but meaningfully impaired.

This is one reason why the counsel to make no major decisions in the first weeks and months after discovery is not a platitude. It is neurologically sound advice.

Why the Body Holds Onto What the Mind Wants to Release

One of the most disorienting aspects of betrayal trauma is the intrusive symptom, the unbidden image, phrase, or memory that arrives with physical force at unexpected moments. For Claire, it was a particular expression she had seen on her husband's face. For others it is a phrase from a text message, the name of the other person, a location, a song that was playing during a relevant period. These intrusions can arrive in the middle of a conversation, during a meeting, in the shower, while driving. They are not chosen. They are not a sign of weakness or obsession. They are a predictable feature of how traumatic memory is encoded.

Under ordinary circumstances, the brain consolidates memories through a process that involves the hippocampus and gradually integrates new information into a broader autobiographical narrative. Traumatic events, however, are encoded differently. High emotional arousal, particularly the kind associated with threat perception, disrupts normal memory consolidation. The amygdala, the brain's threat-evaluation center, becomes hyperactivated and essentially flags the memory as unresolved and unintegrated (van der Kolk, 2014). The result is that these memories are not stored the way ordinary memories are. They are stored in a more fragmented, sensory-dominant way, and they can be retriggered by cues that share perceptual features with the original experience: a smell, a song, a tone of voice, a location.

This is why betrayed partners often describe intrusive experiences as feeling present tense rather than past tense. The nervous system is not replaying a memory so much as re-experiencing a threat signal that has not been resolved. The body has not received confirmation that the danger is over. Until it does, it keeps sending the alert.

Jennifer Freyd's betrayal trauma theory adds another dimension to this. Freyd argues that betrayals by attachment figures, people on whom we depend for safety and care, create a distinctive kind of trauma response because the betrayed person faces a conflict between the psychological need to know the truth and the equally powerful psychological need to maintain the attachment (Freyd, 1996; Freyd & Birrell, 2013). The result, in some cases, is a pattern of reduced awareness or conscious processing of the betrayal, not because the person is in denial exactly, but because full integration of the threat would destabilize the relationship they depend on. When this pattern breaks down, as it does at discovery, the intrusive symptoms often intensify because the suppressed knowledge is flooding the system all at once.

This framework helps explain why some betrayed partners describe not only the shock of discovery but a kind of terrible coherence, a sense that scattered, half-noticed signals from the past are suddenly making a new kind of sense. The body often knew before the mind was willing to integrate what it knew.

* * *

Evan, a forty-seven-year-old high school principal who had been married for twenty-two years when he discovered Amber's affair, described the intrusive symptoms as the thing he was least prepared for. He was a controlled, private man who prided himself on being able to handle difficulty with composure. What he was not prepared for was the way the knowledge kept arriving in his body rather than his mind.

"I'd be standing in front of my staff," he said, "and I'd get a hit of it, like a physical thing, and for about thirty seconds I couldn't remember what I was saying. I'd have to breathe through it. I'd learned to watch myself for it, like you'd watch for a wave coming."

He said that watching for the wave was almost worse than the wave itself: the chronic alertness, the low-grade monitoring, the inability to be fully present in any moment because some part of his attention was always on guard. That monitoring is hypervigilance, and it is one of the most exhausting aspects of betrayal trauma.

Hypervigilance: The Cost of Standing Guard

Hypervigilance is a term from trauma research that refers to a state of chronic elevated alertness in which the nervous system is scanning continuously for signs of threat. It is a common feature of post-traumatic stress responses, and it is nearly universal among people in the acute and middle phases of betrayal trauma (Snyder, Baucom, & Gordon, 2007).

In practical terms, hypervigilance after betrayal looks like this: checking your partner's phone or location without being fully conscious of why you are doing it; noticing the details of your partner's behavior with unusual intensity, tone of voice, micro-expressions, how long they were in another room; scanning conversations for inconsistencies; being unable to be fully present in ordinary moments because you are simultaneously analyzing; feeling a spike of alarm when you cannot immediately reach your partner; interpreting ambiguous signals as potential evidence. None of this is paranoia in any clinical sense. It is an adaptive threat-response that has been triggered by a real event.

The difficulty is that hypervigilance, while understandable, is extraordinarily expensive. The nervous system is not designed for continuous high-alert operation. Chronically elevated vigilance depletes attentional resources, interferes with sleep, impairs concentration, and generates a persistent sense of low-grade dread that makes ordinary daily life feel exhausting in ways that are hard to explain to people who have not experienced it. It also, paradoxically, tends to generate the kind of anxious checking behavior that can make rebuilding trust more difficult over time, not because the checking is unjustified but because it sustains the nervous system's conviction that the danger has not passed.

This is not an argument for premature trust. It is an observation that the nervous system needs concrete safety signals, not just the absence of evidence of ongoing betrayal, to begin downregulating. Those safety signals have to be provided by the unfaithful partner through consistent, transparent, accountable behavior over time, not by the betrayed partner through an act of will. This distinction is critical. You cannot think or decide your way out of hypervigilance. The nervous system changes in response to accumulated experience, not to intentions.

The Attachment System Under Siege

What makes betrayal different from other forms of serious stress is where it originates. The person who hurt you is also, in most cases, the person whose presence your nervous system has learned to associate with safety. This is the specific cruelty of intimate betrayal, and it is rooted in how attachment works.

John Bowlby, whose attachment theory remains foundational across developmental, clinical, and relationship science, described the attachment system as a biological system that evolved to keep us in proximity to people who protect us (Bowlby, 1988). Our primary attachment figures, first our parents, and in adulthood our romantic partners, become what Bowlby called safe havens: sources of comfort and security we turn toward under stress. In healthy attachment relationships, reaching toward your partner when frightened or hurt produces relief. The nervous system has been conditioned, through thousands of accumulated experiences, to associate your partner's presence with safety.

When that person is the source of the threat, the attachment system faces what might fairly be called an impossible situation. The nervous system is simultaneously being driven toward the attachment figure for safety and away from the same person as a source of danger. This conflict generates the profound emotional ambivalence that many betrayed partners describe: wanting to be held by the person who has wounded them, desperately needing closeness while equally needing distance, feeling furious and bereft at the same time. These are not contradictions to be resolved through logic. They are the simultaneous firing of the attachment and threat systems, both behaving exactly as they were designed to behave.

Attachment injuries do not resolve the way ordinary arguments do. They require specific acknowledgment, real accountability, and sustained repair work before the attachment system begins to believe the relationship is safe again. Chapter Eight of this book addresses what that repair work requires in specific, concrete terms. For now, the point is that your nervous system's confusion about where to turn for comfort is not irrational. It is the predictable result of the bond you built being the instrument of your harm.

Grief the Body Carries

Alongside the activation symptoms, hypervigilance, intrusions, sleep disruption, and startle responses, most betrayed partners also experience a grief that can be hard to locate or name. It is not quite the grief of bereavement, though it shares features with it. It is more like the grief of an ongoing, ambiguous loss: the loss of the relationship you believed you had, the loss of a certain version of the future, the loss of your own past as you understood it.

This last element deserves close attention. One of the most disorienting features of betrayal is what researchers have called retroactive re-evaluation: the process by which the discovery of an affair requires the betrayed partner to review and reinterpret a considerable portion of their shared history (Gordon, Baucom, & Snyder, 2004). Moments that seemed ordinary are suddenly shadowed with new and unwanted meaning. Vacations, milestones, ordinary evenings are now uncertain. The betrayed partner finds themselves asking which parts of the past were real.

This is a form of grief with few cultural scripts. Western societies have developed rituals and language for the grief of death. We have far less language for the grief of a living person who has become, in some core way, a stranger, or for the grief of a past that has been revised against your will. The absence of cultural acknowledgment for this kind of loss can leave betrayed partners feeling that their grief is excessive, self-indulgent, or hard to explain, even to themselves. It is none of those things. It is the appropriate response to a multidimensional loss.

Pauline Boss's concept of ambiguous loss is helpful here (Boss, 1999). Boss developed this framework to describe losses that lack the clarity of physical death, situations in which a person is present but fundamentally changed, or absent but psychologically present. Betrayal shares certain features with ambiguous loss: the person you loved is physically there, but the person you thought you knew may feel irrevocably altered. The relationship you believed you had no longer fully exists in the form you understood. This is a substantial loss, and it warrants honest grief. The fact that it does not come with a funeral does not make it less.

Physical Symptoms That Are Not "In Your Head"

Many betrayed partners experience physical symptoms in the weeks and months after discovery, and many of them are embarrassed or confused by these symptoms, particularly if they have no prior history of physical health complaints. These symptoms are real, and they have documented physiological mechanisms.

Sleep disruption is among the most common. The elevated cortisol and the activation of the threat-detection system make it difficult to enter or sustain the relaxed physiological states that sleep requires. Many people describe a specific pattern: falling asleep from exhaustion, waking between 2 and 4 a.m. with the mind immediately engaged on the betrayal, and being unable to return to sleep. This middle-of-the-night waking is associated with cortisol rhythms and is a recognized feature of stress-related sleep disruption (Spiegel, Leproult, & Van Cauter, 1999).

Appetite changes, in both directions, are also common. Some people cannot eat; the sympathetic nervous system activation that accompanies acute stress suppresses appetite by inhibiting the digestive processes. Others eat compulsively as a self-regulation strategy. Neither response reflects poor character. Both are physiological responses to dysregulation.

Immune function can also be affected. Research on psychological stress and immune response has demonstrated that chronic psychosocial stress suppresses immune function in measurable ways (Cohen, Janicki-Deverts, & Miller, 2007). This is part of why betrayed partners are sometimes noticeably more susceptible to illness in the months after discovery.

Physical tension, particularly in the chest, neck, jaw, and shoulders, is reported frequently. Peter Levine, whose work on somatic approaches to trauma has been influential in clinical settings, has written about how unresolved threat responses tend to be held in the body as muscular tension and postural constriction, a kind of physical preparedness that the nervous system maintains when it believes a threat has not been resolved (Levine, 2010). Many betrayed partners describe a sense of physical bracing that they cannot consciously release, a feeling of holding themselves together that is more literal than metaphorical.

Stephen Porges's polyvagal theory adds further texture to the physical picture (Porges, 2011). Porges describes three states of the autonomic nervous system: a ventral vagal state associated with safety, social engagement, and calm; a sympathetic activation state associated with mobilization and fight-or-flight; and a dorsal vagal state associated with immobilization, shutdown, and dissociation. Betrayal can move people through all three states, sometimes within a single day. The social engagement system goes offline under threat, which is why many betrayed partners find it suddenly difficult to be present in ordinary social interaction, to read faces accurately, or to feel truly connected even to people they trust. The flatness, the sense of disconnection, and the difficulty tracking conversation are not personality changes. They are the predictable effects of a nervous system that has been pulled away from its safety state.

It is important to understand that not every betrayed partner will experience all of these symptoms, or will experience them with the same intensity. Individual differences in nervous system baseline, prior trauma history, the severity and duration of the betrayal, the level of ongoing threat or uncertainty in the situation, and the availability of support all influence the specific shape of the trauma response. Some people will be more flooded; others will be more numb. Some will struggle primarily with intrusions; others will experience a pervasive shutdown. Some will have acute symptoms that resolve relatively quickly once the situation stabilizes; others will carry serious symptoms for a year or more.

None of these variations reflect the degree to which you were hurt, or the quality of your character, or how well you are handling things. They reflect the complexity of individual neurobiology encountering a complex stressor.

The Shame Layer

There is one more dimension of the body's response to betrayal that deserves careful attention, because it is among the most painful and least talked about.

Many betrayed partners, alongside the grief and anger, also carry a substantial and disorienting load of shame. This shame is not logical, and most people know it is not logical, but it persists anyway. It takes forms like: What did I miss that I should have seen? What did I do, or fail to do, that contributed to this? What does this say about my worth as a partner, as a person? Why wasn't I enough?

The shame of betrayal is particularly difficult because it attaches to the person who was harmed, not the person who caused the harm. Researchers who study shame and humiliation have noted that betrayal carries a public dimension, even when it is entirely private, because the betrayed partner's sense of how they are seen by their partner, and by themselves, has been damaged (Tangney & Dearing, 2002). The betrayal sends a false message: that you were not sufficient, not interesting enough, not desirable enough, not worth faithfulness.

That message is false. It needs to be said clearly: the unfaithful partner's choice to pursue another relationship is a statement about the unfaithful partner's choices, character, and internal state, not a referendum on the betrayed partner's worth. It bears repeating again, affairs are not caused by the inadequacy of the betrayed spouse. They are caused by the choices of the person who had them. The research on why people have affairs points consistently to factors internal to the unfaithful partner, not to deficiencies in their spouse (Atkins, Baucom, & Jacobson, 2001; Blow & Hartnett, 2005).

But knowing this intellectually and feeling it are different things, and the shame often persists even when the logic is clear. This is because shame is not primarily a cognitive experience. It is a relational and embodied one, and argument rarely dislodges it; honest attunement does, being truly seen and not found wanting, relationships in which you are met with warmth rather than judgment. If you are carrying shame alongside the grief and the anger, that is a normal response to an abnormal situation. It does not require you to earn your way out of it. It requires others to show up honestly with you in it.

If you are reading this in isolation, without anyone who knows what has happened, the shame may feel especially heavy, because there is no relational context in which to set it down. If that is where you are, please hear this: carrying this alone does not mean you should carry it alone. It means the circumstances of your life, perhaps a partner who has demanded silence, a community that cannot hold complexity, a fear of judgment or exposure, have not yet provided you with a safe place to be known. That is a true deprivation. It is not a permanent condition, even though it may feel like one.

Flooding, Numbing, and the Space Between

John Gottman's research on couples in conflict introduced the concept of emotional flooding, a physiological state of overwhelm in which the autonomic nervous system becomes so activated that effective communication and problem-solving become essentially impossible (Gottman, 1994). During flooding, heart rate rises above approximately ninety-five beats per minute for many people, and the capacity for empathy, perspective-taking, and nuanced communication deteriorates sharply. In highly charged marital conflicts, flooding is an obstacle to productive conversation.

In betrayal, flooding is not merely an obstacle to productive conversation. It is a nearly constant companion for many people in the acute phase.

When a betrayed partner tries to have a conversation with their spouse about the affair, and they find themselves unable to stay in the conversation, they are not failing at communication. They are likely flooded, their nervous system overwhelmed by the combination of attachment threat, acute grief, anger, and the relentless demand to process material that is far more than most nervous systems can handle in real time. Asking a flooded person to have a productive, nuanced conversation about the affair is roughly analogous to asking someone in the middle of an asthma attack to run a mile. The capacity is not there. The body is otherwise occupied.

Numbing is the other end of the same spectrum. Some people, rather than flooding, experience a kind of emotional anesthesia in the initial period: a flat affect, a sense of unreality, difficulty accessing feelings that should logically be present. This is dissociation in a mild form, and it is a protective response. The nervous system, faced with material it cannot immediately process, creates a buffer. The feelings are not absent. They are inaccessible, which is different, and they tend to emerge, sometimes intensely, once the immediate shock has stabilized.

Many betrayed partners move between flooding and numbing in ways that feel chaotic and confusing. One day they are devastated, the next day they feel strangely calm, and then something small, a song, a familiar restaurant, an ordinary Tuesday, suddenly breaks them open again. This is not emotional instability. This is the normal oscillation between the pain of confronting the loss and the self-protective impulse to step back from it. Stroebe and Schut's dual process model of grief describes exactly this pattern: healthy grief involves moving back and forth between confronting the loss and orienting toward restoration, and this oscillation is not a sign that something is wrong (Stroebe & Schut, 1999).

The movement is not linear. There is no clean progression from worse to better. There are days of forward movement and days that feel like full regression, and both are part of the same process. The regression is not evidence that healing is not happening. It is frequently a sign that the nervous system is processing something it was not yet ready to process before.

What Your Body Needs, Even Now

This chapter has spent considerable time describing what has gone wrong in the body's response to betrayal trauma. It is equally important to say what can help.

The nervous system changes in response to experience. The same neuroplasticity that allowed it to be shaped by the experience of betrayal also allows it to be reshaped by experiences of safety, regulation, and honest care. This does not happen quickly. It does not happen by decision. But it does happen. Several things matter.

Physical safety is foundational. If you are in a situation where ongoing deception, coercion, emotional manipulation, or any form of abuse is present, your nervous system has an accurate read on the threat level. No amount of coping skill will compensate for actual continued threat. Physical and emotional safety must be addressed before any of the nervous system's deeper responses can begin to shift. If you are not yet safe, the most important question is not how to manage your symptoms. It is how to establish conditions in which safety is present.

Physical care matters more than it may feel like it does. Sleep, even imperfect and irregular sleep, matters. Eating, even when appetite is absent. Movement, not as performance or discipline, but as a way of metabolizing the stress hormones that the body has been generating. Bessel van der Kolk, whose work on trauma and the body has been widely read, notes that the body holds the residue of unresolved trauma, and that physical practices, movement, breath, intentional body awareness, can access and begin to discharge what purely cognitive approaches cannot reach (van der Kolk, 2014). This does not require formal exercise or discipline. Even walking, even brief and irregular walks, provides a physiological pathway for processing that sitting with your thoughts does not.

Connection with safe others is among the most powerful nervous system regulators known. James Coan's work on social baseline theory demonstrates that the nervous system's threat calculations change measurably in the presence of trusted others: the brain literally assesses risk differently when a safe person is nearby (Coan & Sbarra, 2015). If you have even one person with whom you can be honest, not performing, not explaining, simply known, the value of that relationship to your nervous system is not sentimental. It is neurological.

If you do not yet have that person, finding one, through a skilled therapist, a carefully chosen support community, or a trusted friend who can be trusted with this, is not a luxury. It is part of the work. Healing is not a solo enterprise. The nervous system did not evolve for isolation, and trauma that happened in relationship tends to need relationship to resolve.

Finally, and this may be the hardest thing to sit with: you need time. Not indefinite time. Not passive, waiting time. The nervous system needs real time to accumulate a new base of experience. Even when circumstances have been addressed, even when your partner is accountable and truly present, even when the external situation has stabilized, the body takes longer than the mind to update its assessment. The body is not being irrational. It is being appropriately careful. Your nervous system watched the previous assessment be catastrophically wrong, and it is not in a hurry to make that mistake again. This is not a sentence. It is a season. And seasons move.

A Word About Faith and the Body

For readers who hold a faith tradition, there is sometimes an implicit pressure to transcend the body's responses through spiritual effort: to pray past the intrusions, to choose trust, to refuse the anxiety by act of will. This pressure can come from within, from a sincere desire to respond to suffering in ways consistent with one's faith, or it can come from outside, from well-meaning community members or advisors who interpret physical and emotional distress as spiritual failure. This pressure is harmful, and it misunderstands both the body and the nature of authentic spiritual work.

The psalms of the Hebrew Bible are not documents of composed spiritual confidence. They are documents of honest physical and emotional extremity, voices crying from distress, from a sense of being surrounded by enemies, from exhaustion and grief and even from moments of rage. The psalter does not instruct the sufferer to feel differently than they feel. It models the practice of bringing exactly what is present, in all its rawness, into honest address with God. Walter Brueggemann's work on the psalms of disorientation makes this argument with care: lament is not the absence of faith. It is, in the psalter's own witness, a form of faith that refuses to offer God a more presentable version of reality than the one being lived (Brueggemann, 1984; Tanner, 2025).

Dallas Willard's writing on the spiritual life also offers a useful corrective here. Willard was deeply skeptical of what he called the gospel of sin management, the reduction of the spiritual life to behavior management without transformation of the inner person. Authentic spiritual formation, in Willard's account, involves the whole person, including the body, the emotions, and the social self, not merely the will and the intellect (Willard, 1998). This means that attending to what is happening in your body after betrayal, taking it seriously, getting appropriate help for it, and not demanding that you perform a spiritual equanimity you do not possess, is not a failure of faith. It may be the beginning of authentic formation.

The grace available in suffering is not the grace of bypassing the suffering. It is something offered in and through it. That is a slower and harder truth than most of us would choose. But it is closer to the honest witness of both the tradition and the research on human resilience.

The body's response to betrayal is not a malfunction. It is a sophisticated threat-response that has been appropriately triggered by a real and serious threat. The nervous system activates the HPA axis, releases cortisol, generates intrusive symptoms through amygdala-driven memory processes, creates hypervigilance as a threat-monitoring strategy, and produces the profound ambivalence of the attachment system's simultaneous drive toward and away from the source of danger. The grief is real, the shame is understandable, the flooding and numbing are predictable, and the nonlinear movement between states is a feature of healthy trauma processing, not a sign of emotional instability. Your body is not betraying you. It is trying to protect you.

Understanding that distinction will not immediately make the symptoms less disruptive. But it may change the quality of your relationship with them. You are not losing your mind. You are having a documented, describable, ultimately survivable response to a profound relational rupture. Knowing that does not make it easier. But it makes it less alone.

Looking Ahead

Everything described in this chapter, the dysregulation, the physical symptoms, the hypervigilance, the shame that does not belong to you, is happening inside a context. And the most important thing about that context is whether it is safe. The nervous system cannot begin the long work of recovery in an environment that is still actively threatening. Chapter Four addresses the question that must come before almost everything else in this book: what does safety require, how do you assess whether you have it, and what to do when you do not. It is not a comfortable chapter. It is a necessary one.

References

Arnsten, A. F. T. (2009). Stress signalling pathways that impair prefrontal cortex structure and function. *Nature Reviews Neuroscience*, 10(6), 410–422. https://doi.org/10.1038/nrn2648

Atkins, D. C., Baucom, D. H., & Jacobson, N. S. (2001). Understanding infidelity: Correlates in a national random sample. *Journal of Family Psychology*, 15(4), 735–749. https://doi.org/10.1037/0893-3200.15.4.735

Blow, A. J., & Hartnett, K. (2005). Infidelity in committed relationships II: A substantive review. *Journal of Marital and Family Therapy*, 31(2), 217–233. https://doi.org/10.1111/j.1752-0606.2005.tb01556.x

Boss, P. (1999). *Ambiguous loss: Learning to live with unresolved grief.* Harvard University Press.

Bowlby, J. (1988). *A secure base: Parent-child attachment and healthy human development.* Basic Books.

Brueggemann, W. (1984). *The message of the Psalms: A theological commentary.* Augsburg.

Coan, J. A., & Sbarra, D. A. (2015). Social baseline theory: The social regulation of risk and effort. *Current Opinion in Psychology*, 1, 87–91. https://doi.org/10.1016/j.copsyc.2014.12.021

Cohen, S., Janicki-Deverts, D., & Miller, G. E. (2007). Psychological stress and disease. *JAMA*, 298(14), 1685–1687. https://doi.org/10.1001/jama.298.14.1685

Eisenberger, N. I., & Lieberman, M. D. (2004). Why rejection hurts: A common neural alarm system for physical and social pain. *Trends in Cognitive Sciences*, 8(7), 294–300. https://doi.org/10.1016/j.tics.2004.05.010

Eisenberger, N. I., Lieberman, M. D., & Williams, K. D. (2003). Does rejection hurt? An fMRI study of social exclusion. *Science*, 302(5643), 290–292. https://doi.org/10.1126/science.1089134

Freyd, J. J. (1996). *Betrayal trauma: The logic of forgetting childhood abuse.* Harvard University Press.

Freyd, J. J., & Birrell, P. J. (2013). *Blind to betrayal: Why we fool ourselves we aren't being fooled.* Wiley.

Gordon, K. C., Baucom, D. H., & Snyder, D. K. (2004). An integrative intervention for promoting recovery from extramarital affairs. *Journal of Marital and Family Therapy*, 30(2), 213–231. https://doi.org/10.1111/j.1752-0606.2004.tb01235.x

Gottman, J. M. (1994). *What predicts divorce? The relationship between marital processes and marital outcomes.* Lawrence Erlbaum.

Johnson, S. M., Makinen, J. A., & Millikin, J. W. (2001). Attachment injuries in couple relationships: A new perspective on impasses in couples therapy. *Journal of Marital and Family Therapy*, 27(2), 145–155. https://doi.org/10.1111/j.1752-0606.2001.tb01152.x

Levine, P. A. (2010). *In an unspoken voice: How the body releases trauma and restores goodness.* North Atlantic Books.

McEwen, B. S. (2007). Physiology and neurobiology of stress and adaptation: Central role of the brain. *Physiological Reviews*, 87(3), 873–904. https://doi.org/10.1152/physrev.00041.2006

Porges, S. W. (2011). *The polyvagal theory: Neurophysiological foundations of emotions, attachment, communication, and self-regulation.* Norton.

Sapolsky, R. M. (2004). *Why zebras don't get ulcers* (3rd ed.). Holt Paperbacks.

Snyder, D. K., Baucom, D. H., & Gordon, K. C. (2007). *Getting past the affair: A program to help you cope, heal, and move on—together or apart.* Guilford Press.

Spiegel, K., Leproult, R., & Van Cauter, E. (1999). Impact of sleep debt on metabolic and endocrine function. *The Lancet*, 354(9188), 1435–1439. https://doi.org/10.1016/S0140-6736(99)01376-8

Stroebe, M., & Schut, H. (1999). The dual process model of coping with bereavement: Rationale and description. *Death Studies*, 23(3), 197–224. https://doi.org/10.1080/074811899201046

Tangney, J. P., & Dearing, R. L. (2002). *Shame and guilt.* Guilford Press.

Tanner, M. N. (2025). *Finding hope in the ashes: Lament, healing, and the God who stays.* HealingChoice Publishing.

van der Kolk, B. A. (2014). *The body keeps the score: Brain, mind, and body in the healing of trauma.* Viking.

Willard, D. (1998). *The divine conspiracy: Rediscovering our hidden life in God.* HarperCollins

Part 2: Before You Can Move

Chapter Four: Before You Can Heal: The Question of Safety

Claire

Three weeks after she discovered the affair, Claire sat across from her husband at dinner and watched him talk. He was explaining something, something about his workday, or a bill that needed to be paid and she found herself studying him the way you study a stranger. She could hear his voice. She could see his face. But she could not find the person she had thought she knew.

She had not told anyone yet. She had gone to work every day. She had answered emails. She had made meals. And every night, after her husband fell asleep, she lay awake in the dark with a question that would not leave her alone: Is it still happening?

She did not know how to ask him. She was not sure she could trust the answer. And she was not sure, even if she asked and he answered, whether the answer would tell her what she needed to know.

That question — *Is it still happening?* — is not a small question. It is the threshold question of the entire recovery process. And until there is a credible, verifiable answer to it, almost nothing else in this book can take root.

Evan

Three weeks after he found the messages, Evan made a list. He was an administrator by training and by disposition, a person who managed complex institutions by breaking problems into their component parts, identifying what was known and what was not, and moving systematically from uncertainty toward clarity. He had been doing this for twenty years. It was, his assistant principal had once told him the thing that made him good at the job.

He sat at his desk on a Sunday evening, the house quiet, and wrote down what he knew. The affair had lasted three years, or at least three years was what Amber had told him. It had been with a man named Paul who worked in her department. It had begun, according to her, after a conference. It had been, she said, purely physical. It had ended, she said, before he found the messages.

Then he wrote down what he did not know. The actual start date. The actual end date. Whether the end date she had given him was accurate. Whether "purely physical" was the complete account. Whether she had told Paul it was over. Whether they still communicated.

The second list was longer than the first. He was a man who made decisions based on complete information, and he did not have complete information. He did not know how to evaluate anything, whether to stay, whether to believe her, whether the marriage he thought he had been living in had been the marriage that was actually happening, without a baseline of facts that Amber had so far not provided. He had asked. She had answered. But her answers kept containing smaller answers inside them, like nested boxes that, when opened, revealed another box rather than the thing itself.

The question "Is it still happening?" was not, for him, a question about the affair. He was fairly certain the affair was over. The question was whether the deception was still happening. Whether the account he had been given was the account. He did not know how to feel safe inside a story that kept turning out to be shorter than the reality. He closed the notebook. He went to bed. He did not sleep.

* * *

Why Safety Comes First

If you have read the previous chapters, you have begun to understand what betrayal does to the nervous system, to the attachment bond, and to the body's most basic threat-detection systems. You have learned why you cannot think clearly, sleep soundly, or trust your own perceptions the way you once did. You have learned why the mind keeps looping back to the same images, the same questions, the same moments of uncertainty. What you may not yet fully appreciate is that none of that is going to stabilize, let alone heal, in an environment that remains genuinely unsafe.

Safety, in the context of affair recovery, is a concrete and particular thing. It means the affair has ended. It means the contact between your partner and the affair partner has stopped. It means you are receiving honest, consistent information rather than managed disclosures, strategic omissions, or carefully crafted half-truths. It means the deception that was the environment of your life for months or years is not still ongoing.

Research on trauma recovery is consistent on this point: healing requires an environment that the nervous system can gradually learn to experience as safe. Bessel van der Kolk, whose work on trauma has shaped the field for decades, describes the nervous system's recovery as fundamentally dependent on the reduction of ongoing threat (van der Kolk, 2014). When the threat continues, when the affair partner is still a contact in your partner's phone, when you have received a partial disclosure that you sense is partial, when your partner's behavior still carries the markers of concealment, your nervous system cannot afford to begin the work of recovery. It is still in the business of survival.

This is not a character flaw. This is biology. The part of your brain responsible for detecting social and relational danger does not turn off because your partner says the affair is over, or because a well-meaning friend tells you it is time to move forward, or because you have decided, consciously and sincerely, that you want to try to heal. The threat-detection system requires evidence, accumulated over time, before it begins to relax. And if the evidence is not there or if the evidence is actively contradicted it will not relax, no matter how much you want it to.

This chapter is about what genuine safety looks like, why the absence of safety is not your failure, how to begin assessing whether the conditions for recovery exist in your situation, and what honest next steps look like when they do not.

What Safety Is Not

The word "safety" gets used loosely in our culture, and in this context it does not mean several things you might assume. Safety does not mean that you feel comfortable. In the early weeks and months after discovery, you will likely feel uncomfortable regardless of what your partner does. The nervous system that has been through betrayal trauma does not return to baseline quickly. Expecting to feel comfortable before you decide anything about your marriage is not a reasonable standard, and it is not what this chapter is asking you to achieve.

Safety does not mean that the pain has stopped. Pain after betrayal is normal and expected. It will persist for a long time regardless of how safe your environment becomes. Pain is not the same as ongoing danger.

Safety does not mean that your partner has become perfectly trustworthy. Trust is rebuilt incrementally over an extended period of time, and that process belongs in later chapters of this book. What we are discussing here is something more basic: whether the conditions exist under which trust-building is even possible.

And safety does not mean certainty. You may never have absolute certainty about what happened, what your partner is capable of, or what the future holds. Some degree of uncertainty is a permanent feature of life in close relationships, including healthy close relationships. What we are looking for is not certainty but something more modest: a reasonable, evidence-based basis for believing that the deception has stopped. With those misreadings cleared, we can say what safety in this context does require.

What Safety Actually Requires

In practice, safety in the aftermath of betrayal tends to require several concrete things. Not all of them will be in place immediately. Some take time to establish. But they are worth naming clearly, because they give you something real to assess rather than simply asking yourself the unanswerable question of whether you feel safe.

The affair has ended — and the contact has ended

These are not the same thing, and the distinction matters. It is possible for an affair to "end" in name while the emotional or communicative connection between the two people continues. It is possible for your partner to stop the sexual relationship while maintaining a friendship, a professional relationship, or a digital connection with the affair partner. It is possible, and distressingly common, for a partner to believe they have ended an affair that has in fact continued in attenuated form.

From a trauma and nervous system perspective, partial no-contact is not safety. Your body will detect inconsistency in your partner's behavior even before your conscious mind can articulate what it is noticing. You may find yourself checking your partner's phone and not knowing exactly why. You may notice a change in your partner's demeanor after certain calls or messages and not be able to name what feels off. These are not signs of irrationality. These are signs of a nervous system doing exactly what it designed to do.

What genuine no-contact looks like will vary depending on circumstances, especially if the affair partner is a coworker, a mutual friend, or someone your partner cannot realistically never encounter again. In those cases, the standard is not zero contact but rather transparent, limited, and agreed-upon contact. Your partner should be forthcoming about when contact occurs, what was said, and what the purpose was. Secrecy around the affair partner, in any form, is not compatible with safety.

A note on social media and digital contact: this is an area that has become considerably more complicated in the last decade. The mechanisms by which affairs are maintained and re-ignited have multiplied. If your partner maintains a digital connection with the affair partner, follows them, is followed by them, is connected on platforms that allow private messaging, that connection is not trivially insignificant. Reasonable transparency in this area is not an unreasonable thing to ask.

Disclosure is honest and relatively complete

Partial disclosure is one of the most painful and disorienting features of the post-discovery period, and it is far more common than many people realize. The phenomenon, sometimes called "trickle truth" in clinical settings, and documented as "staggered disclosure" in the research literature, refers to the incremental, reactive release of information: revealing details only when the betrayed partner finds them, guesses them, or presses for them. Each new revelation resets the traumatic response and erodes the foundation of trust that the couple is supposedly trying to rebuild (Corley & Schneider, 2002; Snyder, Baucom, & Gordon, 2007). Every piece of information that comes out only because you discovered it or forced it is another piece of evidence that the disclosure process was being managed, not offered.

This does not mean you need to know every detail of every encounter. The research on what is helpful versus harmful in disclosure is genuinely nuanced, and a good therapist can help you think through what information you need for your healing versus what information might be additionally traumatizing without adding clarity. There is a meaningful difference, however, between thoughtful, agreed-upon limits on detail and strategic minimization designed to protect the unfaithful partner's image or the relationship's short-term stability.

If you have the persistent sense that you are not being told the whole truth, if your partner's account keeps shifting, if the details don't quite add up, if you ask a direct question and receive an answer that answers a different question, that sense deserves to be taken seriously. Betrayed spouses frequently know more than their partners think they know. Your intuitions about incomplete disclosure are not, in most cases, paranoia. They are pattern-recognition.

Your partner is in contact with reality about the harm caused

This one is harder to assess, and it unfolds over time. But it matters, because a partner who minimizes the harm of the affair, who is primarily focused on the inconvenience of your pain, who meets your distress with defensiveness, who subtly or explicitly suggests that your reaction is excessive, that partner is not creating a safe environment for your healing.

Safety requires that your pain be acknowledged as real and serious. It requires that your partner demonstrate, at least in basic ways, an understanding that something substantial was done. It does not require that your partner be a perfectly empathetic, completely non-defensive, therapeutically sophisticated presence. People in the early stages of coming to terms with what they have done are often flooded with shame, guilt, defensiveness, and self-protective responses. Some of that is normal. But there is a difference between a partner who is struggling with shame and a partner who is managing your perception of what happened.

Gottman's research on what makes repair possible in the aftermath of betrayal points to this distinction clearly. Remorse, honest acknowledgment of the harm, accompanied by the expressed desire to make it right is foundational to the repair process (Gottman & Silver, 1999). Without it, the repair framework has nothing to attach to.

You have some degree of physical and emotional safety

This should go without saying, but it bears saying: physical safety is not negotiable. If there is any element of physical intimidation, coercion, or abuse in your relationship, including coercive control, financial control, isolation, or threatening behavior, that is a different and more urgent situation than the one this book primarily addresses. Please reach out to a domestic violence advocate or a trained therapist who specializes in abuse dynamics before working through this material. The framework of affair recovery assumes a baseline of physical safety. Where that baseline does not exist, the question is not how to repair the relationship but how to protect yourself.

Emotional safety is more complex and less absolute. Some degree of emotional volatility, from both partners is normal and expected in the early months after discovery. But a pattern in which your partner's anger, withdrawal, threats, contempt, or emotional volatility are consistently used to shut down your questions, silence your distress, or prevent you from making clear-eyed assessments of your situation is not a safe environment. You should be able to ask questions. You should be able to feel what you feel. You should be able to have conversations about the affair, difficult as they are, without the conversation being weaponized against you.

When Safety Is Not Yet Present

Reading this chapter, you may have found yourself mentally noting, one by one, the ways in which the conditions above are not yet in place in your situation. If so, this section is written for you.

The absence of safety is not a verdict on your marriage. It is not a verdict on whether repair is possible. And it is not, in any way, a reflection on your worth, your adequacy, or your judgment. What it is, honestly, is a serious obstacle, one that needs to be named clearly before any meaningful progress can happen. There are several different scenarios worth distinguishing here.

Scenario One: Ongoing deception you can sense but cannot yet prove

This is one of the most disorienting positions a betrayed spouse can be in. You have a persistent sense that the affair is not fully over, or that you are not getting the complete truth, but you cannot point to definitive evidence. Your partner is telling you it is over. Perhaps others are telling you it is over. And yet something in you remains unconvinced.

If you are in this position, do not dismiss what you are noticing. As discussed earlier in this book, betrayed spouses often detect ongoing deception through very subtle behavioral cues long before they have explicit evidence. Your nervous system is not malfunctioning. Your uncertainty does not mean you are paranoid.

In this situation, two things are true simultaneously: you deserve honesty, and you also deserve support from someone who can help you assess what you are experiencing with greater clarity. A skilled therapist, particularly one with experience in affair recovery can help you distinguish between trauma-driven hypervigilance and legitimate threat-detection. Both are real. Both deserve attention. They just require different responses.

A trained therapist can also help you figure out what questions to ask your partner and how to ask them in ways that are more likely to produce honest responses. And if the responses you receive continue to feel incomplete or inconsistent, that information itself is meaningful.

Scenario Two: Your partner has ended the affair but is not engaging with the repair process

Some unfaithful partners end the affair but then seem to expect that the relationship will return more or less to its previous state. They want the marriage to survive, but they are not willing to do the specific work that recovery requires: the transparency, the answering of questions, the consistent accountability, the tolerating of your pain without deflecting, the investment in a therapeutic process.

This is a common and painful position. The affair may truly be over. Your partner may not be a malicious person. But without engagement in the recovery process, the wound does not close. The betrayed spouse is left holding all of the pain and all of the work, while the unfaithful partner gradually returns to normal or becomes increasingly impatient with the fact that normal has not yet returned.

If this is your situation, this book can still offer you substantial support for your own stabilization and healing. What it cannot offer is a substitute for the work that requires both partners. At some point, and you will know when, you will need to have a frank conversation with your partner about what real repair requires. Chapter Seven of this book is largely written for unfaithful partners and may be a useful resource in that conversation.

Scenario Three: You are not yet sure whether the affair has ended

Some readers are in a situation in which they genuinely do not know whether the affair has ended, because the full picture has not yet been established, because their partner has made promises whose credibility is unclear, or because discovery is still recent and the facts have not stabilized.

In this situation, the most important thing is to resist the pressure to make premature decisions. You do not have to decide whether to stay or leave this week. You do not have to decide whether to forgive yet. You do not have to perform stability you do not feel. What you do need to do is gather information, establish clarity as much as possible, and attend to your own immediate wellbeing while the picture becomes clearer.

This process, establishing what happened, with whom, for how long, and what the current status is, is not just a practical necessity. It is also, for many betrayed spouses, an important part of their own psychological and emotional recovery. The need to know is real and should be treated as legitimate, not as excessive curiosity or self-torture. You experienced something in your marriage. You have a right to understand what it was.

The Role of Professional Support

Here is what needs to be said directly about therapy, because the presence or absence of professional support makes a real difference in what is possible for you right now.

If you and your partner are in couples therapy with a therapist who has specific training in affair recovery, you have a substantial resource. A skilled therapist can help establish a structured, guided disclosure process, can work with both partners to create conditions of safety, and can provide the containment that allows highly volatile conversations to be productive rather than destructive. I recommend a Certified Gottman Therapist who has training in affair recovery.

If you are in individual therapy, even without your partner, you also have something valuable: a space in which you can think clearly, stabilize, and receive informed support without having to manage your partner's reactions at the same time. Individual therapy for the betrayed spouse is not a consolation prize. It is often the most important single intervention for stabilization.

If you have no therapeutic support at all, this book can serve as an important resource, but it cannot replace what good therapy provides. Betrayed partners do meaningfully better with professional support (Snyder, Castellani, & Whisman, 2006). If access to therapy is a barrier because of cost, availability, or your partner's unwillingness, there may be options worth exploring; community mental health centers, graduate training clinics, online therapy platforms, and support groups oriented toward betrayal trauma. You do not have to navigate this alone, even if that is how it currently feels.

What You Can Do Right Now

Even if full safety is not yet established, there are concrete things you can do to attend to your own stabilization while working toward the conditions that recovery requires.

First, take your perceptions seriously. If something feels wrong, do not dismiss it. Do not manage your own intuitions on your partner's behalf. Your sense that something is incomplete, inconsistent, or continuing is worth attending to, not suppressing.

Second, attend to physical basics. Sleep, food, water, and movement are not trivial in the context of trauma. The nervous system that has been dysregulated by betrayal is partly a body, and the body requires basic care. If you are not sleeping, if you have stopped eating, if you are relying on alcohol or other substances to get through the night, these are not signs of weakness but they are signs that your body needs attention. Basic physical care is not a detour from healing. It is part of it.

Third, identify at least one person you can be honest with. Isolation amplifies the suffering of betrayal trauma. You do not have to tell everyone. You do not have to make public declarations. But carrying this entirely alone, without a single trusted person who knows what is happening in your life, creates a weight that compounds the injury. If no personal confidant feels available to you right now, a therapist, a clergy person you trust, or a support group for betrayed spouses can serve this function.

Fourth, resist the pressure to rush. Both internal and external pressure to resolve this quickly, to decide quickly, to get back to normal quickly, runs directly against what the research tells us about recovery. Healing from betrayal trauma is not a fast process. Meaningful repair takes time. You do not owe anyone a timeline.

Fifth, do not make major decisions under maximum distress. The acute phase of trauma is not the time to sell the house, end the marriage, relocate, or make other major life changes unless those changes are directly necessary for your safety. Many decisions that feel urgent in the first weeks after discovery are not actually time-sensitive. Give yourself some room.

The Courage to See Clearly

What this chapter is asking of you, honestly assessing whether the conditions for safety exist in your situation, requires courage. It is easier, in some ways, to suppress the question, to accept reassurances at face value, to tell yourself that things are probably fine, to focus on the future and not look too closely at the present.

But real healing requires real clarity. You cannot heal from something you are still pretending is not happening. You cannot begin to rebuild trust on a foundation of ongoing deception. And you cannot make a wise decision about your future, whether you stay, whether you go, whether you try to repair, and on what terms, if you do not have a reasonably accurate understanding of where you are.

This kind of clarity takes courage partly because the answers may be painful. There may be things you do not want to know.

There may be truths that, once fully seen, will require difficult decisions. But there is a long-term cost to not looking. The cost is that you end up spending years trying to heal from something that has not fully stopped, or trying to trust a process that was never fully honest, or carrying a weight of unasked questions that eventually becomes too heavy to bear.

Many people who have been through this process say, looking back, that the period of honest assessment, painful as it was, was when their healing began. Not when they received reassurances. Not when they stopped asking questions. When they started asking the right ones, and insisting on real answers.

There is a kind of spiritual wisdom that gets misapplied in the aftermath of betrayal. It sounds like this: be patient, be forgiving, have faith, do not assume the worst. These instincts are not wrong in themselves. But they can be used by others, and by ourselves to suppress legitimate perception, to silence honest grief, and to avoid the hard work of seeing clearly.

Faith, at its best, does not ask you to suppress your perception of reality. The Psalms are full of people who looked at their circumstances with unflinching honesty and said, out loud, this is what is happening to me. This is what has been done to me. This is what I need. That kind of honesty is not a failure of faith. It is a form of it. Lament is not the opposite of trust, it is what trust sounds like when life has broken open.

Dallas Willard wrote about the hardness of heart as one of the deepest forms of spiritual disorder, a condition in which a person has progressively closed themselves to reality, to others, and ultimately to God (Willard, 2002). The hardness of heart that enables betrayal is one expression of this. But there is another kind of hardening that can happen on the other side: the hardening that comes from pretending to feel safe when you are not, from performing trust that has not yet been earned, from managing your own perceptions so that you do not have to ask the hard questions.

God is not honored by that performance. The capacity to see things as they are and to act in light of what you see is not a spiritual failure. It is a precondition for healing that lasts.

You are allowed to ask for clarity. You are allowed to insist on honesty. You are allowed to need more than reassurances. That is not a lack of faith. That is integrity.

Looking Ahead

The next chapter of this book is about the inner landscape of the weeks and months that follow discovery: the flooding, the triggers, the intrusive thoughts, the grief that comes in waves, and what the research tells us about how the nervous system and attachment system begin, slowly, unevenly, to find their footing.

But the chapters ahead, all of them, rest on what this chapter has addressed. Safety is not just one item on a recovery checklist. It is the ground on which everything else is built.

If you are in a situation where safety is present, or where it is being actively and credibly worked toward, you have the most important foundation in place. The road ahead is still long and nonlinear, and there will be hard days. But the conditions exist for real work to begin.

If you are not yet in that situation, the work of this chapter, honest assessment, courageous clarity, wise attention to your own wellbeing is not a pause from recovery. It is recovery. The healing available to you right now is the healing of being clear about where you are. That is not nothing. For many people, it is where everything begins.

References

Corley, M. D., & Schneider, J. P. (2002). Disclosing secrets: Guidelines for therapists working with sex addicts and co-addicts. *Sexual Addiction & Compulsivity*, 9(1), 43–67. https://doi.org/10.1080/107201602317343313

Gottman, J. M., & Silver, N. (1999). *The seven principles for making marriage work*. Crown Publishers.

Snyder, D. K., Baucom, D. H., & Gordon, K. C. (2007). *Getting past the affair: A program to help you cope, heal, and move on—together or apart.* Guilford Press.

Snyder, D. K., Castellani, A. M., & Whisman, M. A. (2006). Current status and future directions in couple therapy. *Annual Review of Psychology*, 57, 317–344. https://doi.org/10.1146/annurev.psych.56.091103.070154

van der Kolk, B. A. (2014). *The body keeps the score: Brain, mind, and body in the healing of trauma.* Viking.

Willard, D. (2002). *Renovation of the heart: Putting on the character of Christ.* NavPress.

Chapter Five: Stay, Leave, or Wait

"Everything can be taken from a man but one thing: the last of the human freedoms—to choose one's attitude in any given set of circumstances, to choose one's own way."
— Viktor Frankl, Man's Search for Meaning (1946/1959)

Claire

Six weeks after discovery, Claire's sister asked her the question everyone eventually asks: So what are you going to do?

Claire had no answer. She was not sure whether she still loved her husband. She was not sure whether she could ever trust him again. She was not sure whether she wanted to try. What she knew was that she was still not sleeping through the night, that the question of whether the affair was fully over had not been answered to her satisfaction, and that the thought of making a permanent decision about the rest of her life felt like being asked to navigate by a compass that had stopped working. She said: I don't know yet. And her sister, meaning well, said: You're going to have to figure it out eventually.

That is true. But "eventually" is doing a great deal of work in that sentence. The pressure to decide, to choose, to resolve, to move in some direction is one of the defining features of the aftermath of betrayal, and it comes from everywhere: from family, from friends, from faith communities, from the unfaithful partner who wants clarity, from your own mind which craves the relief that a decision seems to promise. That pressure deserves careful examination before you do anything else, because the pressure itself is part of what makes this period so disorienting.

This chapter is about the decision that is probably weighing on you most: whether to stay in this relationship, leave it, or hold the question in deliberate suspension while you gather the clarity that any wise decision requires. It does not resolve that question for you. No book can do that. But it can help you understand what a wise process looks like, what the research tells us about timing and outcomes, what the different paths require, and how to distinguish a decision made from clarity from one made under conditions that undermine good judgment.

Evan

No one in his professional life knew. He was a fifty-seven staff members' principal. He ran a building of twelve hundred students. He sat in IEP meetings and school board sessions and parent conferences in which other people's most difficult situations were laid before him for navigation. He was, in those rooms, the person who held things together.

He could not tell those people. And the people he might have told, a handful of friends from graduate school, his brother in Colorado, were people he had learned, over a twenty-two-year marriage, to keep at a certain distance. He had been, he was beginning to understand, a private man to the point of isolation.

Six weeks after discovery, the question arrived from an unexpected direction: not a family member, but his oldest friend from college, a man named Barrett who had driven four hours for a weekend visit and who had sat across from Evan at a restaurant and said, quietly: I don't know what's happening, but something is. You don't have to tell me if you can't. But you should know I'm asking.

Evan had looked at his menu for a moment. Then he had told him. Barrett had not said much. He had asked a few questions. He had not offered advice. At the end of the conversation he had said: So what are you going to do?

Evan said: I don't know yet.

Barrett had nodded and said: That sounds right for right now.

Evan had been waiting, without knowing he was waiting, for someone to say exactly that. The pressure to resolve, to decide, to produce an answer that would let everyone around him relax, including Amber, who wanted to know whether the marriage would survive, not because she was certain she wanted it to but because the uncertainty was painful to manage, had been relentless. The simple acknowledgment that not knowing, right now, was the accurate and appropriate response felt like setting down something he had been carrying for six weeks.

He did not have enough information to decide. He was a man who did not make decisions without complete information. He was beginning to understand that the first task was not the decision. It was the information. And getting the information, in this particular situation, was going to require something he was not sure he had yet: the willingness to press for a truth that Amber, so far, had been supplying in pieces.

* * *

Why the Pressure to Decide Is the First Problem

The urgency that surrounds the post-discovery period is often not proportional to what is time-sensitive. Some decisions are genuinely urgent: if your physical safety is in question, if you are in a financially vulnerable position, if children are being harmed by the immediate environment. Those require prompt action. But the core question of whether this marriage can or should survive is almost never as time-sensitive as it feels in the acute phase of betrayal trauma.

What makes it feel urgent is the nervous system. Trauma activates a drive for resolution that is physiological at its core. The threat-detection system that governs your stress response does not manage ambiguity well. It wants information, certainty, closure. The racing thoughts, the obsessive return to the same questions, the compulsive need to know right now what you are going to do, these are not signs that a decision must be made immediately. They are signs that your nervous system is under severe strain and is seeking relief through the illusion of control.

Gottman and Silver's research on couples in crisis has long emphasized the importance of not making major life decisions under conditions of acute flooding (Gottman & Silver, 1999). The cognitive and emotional impairment that accompanies the flooded state, elevated heart rate, compromised prefrontal access, reduced capacity to hold competing considerations simultaneously, is precisely the state in which most betrayed spouses are asked to decide whether to end or continue a marriage. The resulting decisions are frequently ones people come to regret, not because the decision itself was wrong, but because it was made before the information needed to make it well was available.

The urgency that surrounds the post-discovery period is often not proportional to what is actually time-sensitive.

There is a second source of pressure that deserves naming directly: the unfaithful partner. Many unfaithful partners, after the initial crisis of discovery, become anxious about the uncertainty of their own future. Some of this is real remorse and the desire to know whether repair is possible. But some of it is self-protective urgency, the discomfort of sitting with unresolved guilt and relational instability, and the wish to move quickly toward either reconciliation or resolution. When this urgency is transferred to the betrayed spouse as pressure to decide, it is, whether intended or not, a form of continuing to prioritize the unfaithful partner's comfort over the betrayed spouse's legitimate need for time.

If you are receiving this kind of pressure, name it directly, at least to yourself. You do not owe anyone a timeline for deciding what to do with your own life after it has been profoundly disrupted by someone else's choices.

The Cost of Premature Decision, in Both Directions

Two forms of premature decision-making tend to produce the outcomes that people most regret, and they run in opposite directions.

Staying Before Conditions Exist for Repair

The first is deciding to stay and attempt reconciliation before the conditions that make repair possible are in place. Chapter Four addressed those conditions in detail: the affair has genuinely ended, contact with the affair partner has stopped, disclosure has been honest and relatively complete, and the unfaithful partner is demonstrating real accountability rather than managing perception. When a betrayed spouse decides to stay before those conditions exist, they are not actually beginning recovery. They are continuing to live in the original unsafe environment while calling it something different.

This is one of the most common and most costly patterns in affair recovery. It happens for understandable reasons: the desire to restore normalcy, the pressure from the unfaithful partner or from the surrounding community, the fear of what leaving would mean, the genuine love for the person who caused the harm, the hope that things will improve. None of these motivations are irrational. But the research on recovery trajectories is consistent: couples who attempt repair before the foundational conditions are in place tend to cycle through repeated crises rather than progressing through them, because the underlying breach of safety has never been genuinely addressed (Gordon, Baucom, & Snyder, 2004).

Staying prematurely is not simply an emotional error. It has practical consequences for the healing process. When a betrayed spouse commits to repair before they have enough information to make that commitment from a position of clarity, they often find themselves unable to do the internal work that recovery requires. The grief has not been named. The anger has not been expressed. The questions have not been answered. The conditions for trusting have not been established. And the pressure to perform recovery, to appear healed, to demonstrate that the marriage is intact, can drive the actual experience of the wound underground, where it persists without resolution.

Leaving Before Reaching Clarity

The second form of premature decision-making runs in the other direction. Some betrayed spouses, especially those with anxious or avoidant attachment histories, move quickly toward separation or divorce not from a position of real clarity but from the urgent need to escape the intolerable pain of uncertainty. This is not the same as leaving from a clear-eyed assessment of the situation. It is leaving because staying feels unbearable and doing something feels better than doing nothing.

Decisions made in this register often carry their own regrets. Not because staying would necessarily have been wiser, but because the person who left did so without knowing what they were leaving, without processing the full weight of what happened, and sometimes without the chance to test whether repair was possible or not. They carry the wound with them, unanswered.

This is not an argument against leaving. Leaving is sometimes the clearest and most necessary thing a betrayed spouse can do. There are situations where the affair has not ended, where the unfaithful partner is unwilling to engage repair, where the relationship has never been safe, or where the cumulative evidence of the partnership's history points toward a decision that is better made sooner rather than later. The point is not that leaving is wrong. The point is that leaving, like staying, deserves to be done from a position of information and clarity rather than from acute distress alone.

What Genuine Clarity Requires

If premature decision-making in either direction is the problem, then clarity is the goal. What that means deserves precision, because clarity is often misunderstood as a feeling, a moment when everything suddenly becomes obvious. That kind of clarity rarely comes. What does come, with time and support and honest engagement with the available information, is a more grounded, less reactive, more fully informed basis for making a major life decision. Several things tend to be necessary before that kind of clarity is reachable.

Enough Information

You cannot make a wise decision about this relationship without a reasonably accurate account of what happened in it. If you have not received honest, complete disclosure, the decision you make is not based on reality but on the partial and possibly distorted account you have been given. This matters in both directions:

someone who stays on the basis of an incomplete account may discover later that what they agreed to repair was not what occurred. Someone who leaves on the basis of an incomplete account loses the opportunity to make a fully informed choice.

The need for information is not pathological curiosity or self-torment. It is a precondition for adult decision-making. You have the right to know what happened in your own marriage.

Enough Time

The research on recovery from serious relational trauma consistently indicates that decisions made in the first weeks and months after discovery are less reliable indicators of long-term outcomes than decisions made after the acute phase has passed (Gordon et al., 2004; Spring, 2012). This does not mean decisions must be indefinitely deferred. It means that the window of maximum distress, when the nervous system is most flooded, sleep is most disrupted, and access to complex reasoning is most impaired is not the window in which the most important decisions of your life should be finalized.

How much time is enough? There is no precise answer. What clinicians who specialize in affair recovery observe is that something begins to shift, usually somewhere between three and six months after discovery, when the acute traumatic flooding begins to moderate and the person can access more of their own knowing. That is not a universal rule. It depends on whether safety has been established, whether professional support is available, and whether the situation is continuing to destabilize or has reached some relative equilibrium. But it is a reason to be cautious about treating the urgency of the acute phase as though it reflects the urgency of the actual decision.

Enough Support

Decisions made in isolation are more vulnerable to distortion than decisions made with thoughtful outside perspective. This does not mean your decision should be made by committee. It means that a trusted therapist, a skilled counselor, or even one honest and informed friend can serve as a check on the ways that grief, shame, fear, and hope can each pull a person toward a conclusion that serves the emotion rather than the whole truth of the situation. The research on outcomes in affair recovery is consistent on this point: access to professional or structured support makes a meaningful difference in recovery trajectories (Snyder, Castellani, & Whisman, 2006).

If you have no support at all right now, that is a relevant piece of information about your situation. Carrying this alone, while also being asked to make major life decisions, is a very heavy load. Finding at least one form of informed support, whether individual therapy, a support group for betrayed spouses, or a trusted clergy person with experience in this area is not a luxury. For the purposes of this decision, it is something close to a necessity.

Three Paths, Honestly Described

With those foundations in view, the three broad directions available to you deserve honest description. None of them is the universally correct choice. Each has real costs, real risks, and real possibilities.

Staying and Attempting Repair

Staying in the relationship and committing to a real repair process is the path that requires the most from both partners, carries the longest timeline, and offers the possibility of something that many couples who have been through it describe as more honest and more deeply grounded than what existed before the betrayal. That is not a promise. It is what the research documents in couples who successfully navigate this process.

What makes repair genuinely possible, rather than merely attempted, is the specific set of conditions that have been discussed in Chapter Four and will be developed further in the chapters ahead. In brief: the affair is over, disclosure has been honest and relatively complete, the unfaithful partner is demonstrating honest accountability rather than image management, and both partners are willing to engage a structured process of rebuilding that will require sustained effort over an extended period. Gordon, Baucom, and Snyder's integrative intervention research identifies these conditions as the distinguishing factors between couples whose repair attempts succeed and those that do not (Gordon et al., 2004).

What staying requires of the betrayed spouse specifically, beyond the obvious willingness to try deserves plain acknowledgment. It requires tolerating considerable ongoing uncertainty about whether the effort will succeed. It requires doing difficult internal work, including processing grief and anger that cannot simply be suppressed for the sake of the relationship's stability. It requires being willing to be vulnerable again with a person who has already shown the capacity to harm you. These are not small things, they are real demands rather than minimized in the service of encouraging reconciliation.

Staying is not easier than leaving. In some ways it is harder. The decision to stay should be made because the conditions for repair appear to be present and the relationship is worth the sustained investment, not because staying feels less frightening or because the pressure to preserve the marriage has become too loud to resist.

Leaving the Relationship

Leaving is sometimes the clearest, most necessary, and most self-respecting thing a betrayed spouse can do. There is no universal shame in it and no universal wisdom in it. It depends on what is present in the specific situation.

There are circumstances that make the case for leaving straightforward rather than ambiguous: when the affair has not ended and the unfaithful partner shows no credible intention of ending it; when there is a pattern of repeated betrayal rather than a single event; when the unfaithful partner refuses to engage in any meaningful repair process; when there is ongoing deception, coercion, or abuse; or when an honest assessment of the relationship's history reveals that the foundation for a trustworthy partnership was never established.

Beyond these clearer cases, there are situations where the case for leaving is less clear, where the unfaithful partner is trying, where there is real history and real love, but where the betrayed spouse has reached a clear-eyed assessment that they cannot rebuild trust in this relationship and that continued investment in the attempt would cost more than it returns. That is a legitimate basis for leaving, and it does not require the relationship to be beyond repair in some objective sense. It requires only that the person who was harmed has assessed, as honestly as they are able, that repair is not what they want or need.

Leaving does not end the healing process. It changes its context. The grief, the anger, the attachment injury, the questions that need answering, these persist outside the marriage as well as inside it. Research on recovery trajectories documents that people who leave do heal, but the healing tends to require its own time, its own support, and its own honest engagement with what happened (Spring, 2012). Leaving is not an escape from the work. It is a choice to do the work in a different relational setting.

Deliberate Waiting

The third path rarely gets named as a legitimate option. That is the first reason to name it clearly. Deliberate waiting, holding the decision without making it is not the same as passive avoidance. It is an active choice to remain in suspension while gathering the information, time, and clarity that a wise decision requires.

Deliberate waiting looks like this: you have not decided to stay and commit to repair, and you have not decided to leave. You are in a period of honest assessment. You are paying attention to whether the conditions for repair are developing or not, whether the unfaithful partner's behavior is changing in substantive ways or only in surface ways, whether your own sense of the situation is becoming clearer or more muddled, whether professional support is helping you access your own knowing. You are taking care of your basic stability. You are not pretending to have more resolution than you have.

This is a legitimate place to be, and it deserves protection. The pressure from outside and sometimes from inside to resolve the ambiguity is real and persistent. But ambiguity, held honestly, is preferable to false resolution in either direction. A decision made from real clarity, whenever it arrives, will be more livable than a decision made to escape the discomfort of not yet knowing.

Deliberate waiting is not the same as indefinite waiting. At some point, continuing to hold the question open has its own costs, especially if children are involved, if the emotional volatility of the unresolved situation is preventing both partners from functioning, or if the unfaithful partner's engagement in the repair process cannot be sustained in open-ended limbo. At some point a provisional commitment, or a provisional decision to part, needs to be made. But that point is usually much further away than the acute pressure suggests.

What Complicates the Decision

Several features of most real situations make the stay-leave-wait question considerably more complex than the three paths described above might suggest.

Children

The presence of children does not resolve the decision, but it changes its weight and its shape. The research on children and divorce is considerably more complex than common assumptions suggest, and this is not the place to treat it comprehensively. What can be said is that the notion that staying together for the children is always the right choice has not held up well under empirical scrutiny. Children are harmed by chronic parental conflict, ongoing household instability, and the emotional unavailability of parents who are overwhelmed by unresolved pain, whether the family remains formally intact or not (Amato, 2001).

This is not an argument for or against staying. It is an argument against using the children as a reason to avoid an honest assessment of the situation. Children are best served by honest, stable, emotionally available parents and sometimes that means intact families and sometimes it does not.

Faith and Community

For readers with strong faith commitments, the decision about whether to stay or leave carries weight that extends beyond the relational into the theological and communal. The covenant of marriage is not a trivial concept in most faith traditions, and a faith community's response to betrayal and separation can be either a real source of support or a source of additional pressure that complicates rather than clarifies.

This book holds covenantal commitment seriously. That is the appropriate response to a serious theological framework. But it also holds, without qualification, that covenantal commitment is not properly used as a tool to prevent a betrayed spouse from making an honest assessment of their situation, or to shame them for considering a path that the community would prefer they not take. There is a version of covenant theology that functions as coercion. Call it what it is.

The faith reflection section at the close of this chapter engages this more fully. For now, the point is that faith commitments deserve to be honored in this discernment process not suppressed, but also not used as a substitute for honest assessment.

Financial and Practical Entanglement

Many betrayed spouses are also financially dependent on their partner, co-owners of property, co-parents of children, or otherwise entangled in practical ways that make the decision to leave logistically complex and frightening. This is real and it matters. Financial vulnerability, in particular, can function as a form of coercion, making the option of leaving feel unavailable even when it might otherwise be the clearer choice.

If this is your situation, getting informed is worth the effort. An attorney consultation, even an initial one, can clarify your actual options and what the realities of separation would look like. Information is not the same as commitment. Knowing what is available to you is not the same as deciding to pursue it. But making decisions about staying or leaving while operating from uninformed fear of what leaving would mean is not a good basis for major life choices.

Clarity Versus Fear, Shame, and Pressure

One of the most useful distinctions available to you in this period is the difference between a decision that is emerging from clarity and a decision that is being driven by something else.

Decisions driven by fear tend to be oriented toward the avoidance of a specific outcome rather than toward what is true and good. They are often characterized by urgency, by a narrowing of perspective, by the sense that one particular path is the only way to make the pain stop. Decisions driven by shame tend to be oriented toward managing others' perceptions: staying to avoid the stigma of divorce, or leaving to appear strong and self-respecting in a way that suppresses more ambivalent truth. Decisions driven by external pressure tend to substitute others' certainty for one's own.

None of these are illegitimate emotional experiences. Fear, shame, and responsiveness to community are human and normal. But they are not good primary navigators for a decision of this magnitude.

Decisions emerging from honest clarity tend to have different characteristics. They come with some spaciousness rather than only urgency. They can hold more than one consideration at a time. They acknowledge complexity rather than collapsing it. They feel more like an honest reckoning than a desperate resolution. They do not necessarily feel painless or easy. But they feel true in a way that pressure-driven decisions rarely do.

This distinction is not always obvious in the moment. It often becomes visible only in retrospect, or with the help of a good therapist who can reflect back what they are hearing. Cultivating awareness of it is worth the effort, because it is one of the most reliable guides available to you right now.

A Word to Readers in Specific Situations

This chapter has been written for a range of readers, and a few specific situations deserve a direct word.

If the Affair Has Not Ended

If you have reason to believe the affair is still ongoing, whether because you have direct evidence, because your partner's account does not cohere, or because the behavioral signals you are reading have not changed then you are not in a position to make a decision about repair. You are still in a position of ongoing harm. The work of this moment is not discernment about the future of the marriage. It is the work of establishing the truth of the present. That is a different and more urgent task.

This does not mean you must leave immediately. It means that any apparent decision to stay and try to repair is provisional until the basic question of whether the affair has ended can be answered with reasonable confidence. You do not owe anyone, including yourself, a final answer while the fundamental facts are still unclear.

If You Are Being Pressured

If your partner, your family, your pastor, or your community are actively pressuring you to make a decision on their timeline rather than yours, name that directly, at least to yourself. The pressure may be well-intentioned. The people applying it may sincerely believe they are helping. But a major life decision made under pressure tends to be a decision made for the benefit of the people applying the pressure rather than for the benefit of the person making it. You have the right to your own process, including its pace.

If You Are Completely Alone in This

Some readers are carrying this without a single person who knows what is happening. No therapist, no trusted friend, no family member who can be told. If that is you, the isolation you are experiencing is itself a form of harm, even if it is self-imposed for reasons that make complete sense. You cannot make this decision optimally alone, not because you lack the capacity for good judgment, but because the conditions that support good judgment, honest reflection, outside perspective, the ability to speak what you are experiencing to someone who will bear witness to it are not available to you.

Finding one form of support, even an imperfect one, is worth the effort. Online support communities for betrayed spouses, telephone-based therapy, community mental health resources are not ideal substitutes for good in-person therapeutic support, but they are better than none. You deserve to make this decision with some form of informed human presence alongside you.

A Reflection: Covenant, Commitment, and the Courage to See Clearly

For readers who hold faith commitments, the question of whether to stay, leave, or wait arrives inside a framework that is not neutral. Marriage, in most serious theological traditions, is a covenant relationship which means it carries a weight and a seriousness that ordinary contracts do not. That weight is real, and it deserves to be honored rather than dismissed.

But there is a version of covenantal reasoning that has been misapplied in the context of betrayal, sometimes with real harm. It sounds like this: because you made a vow, you must stay. Because you made a vow, you must forgive on a fixed timeline. Because you made a vow, your feelings about what was done to you are less important than the preservation of the institution. Because you made a vow, asking hard questions is a failure of faith.

Dallas Willard's framework for understanding covenant is instructive here. Covenant, in his reading, is not primarily a legal obligation but a structure for soul formation, a context in which two people agree to become, over time, the kind of people who love each other well (Willard, 2002). That framework takes commitment seriously. It does not treat vows as trivial. But it also recognizes that covenant requires the participation of both people. A covenant in which one person has systematically deceived the other is a covenant already broken at its core. Calling the betrayed spouse to honor their vow as though the other partner had honored theirs requires a kind of spiritual accounting that does not add up.

This does not mean covenant commitment provides no guidance in this discernment. It means it provides a different kind of guidance than the coercive version assumes. A covenantal framework that is functioning correctly asks: what does genuine love require here? What does integrity require? What does the long-term formation of both people, not just the preservation of the external structure call for? Those are harder and more honest questions than simply: what does staying require of you?

Wherever this process leads you, you can bring your faith into it honestly. You do not have to choose between taking your vows seriously and taking your own safety and dignity seriously. A theology that asks you to make that choice has already made an error.

* * *

Claire eventually answered her sister's question. Not that day, and not the way her sister had expected.

What she said was this: I'm not ready to decide yet. But I'm not staying because I'm afraid to leave, and I'm not leaving because I'm afraid to stay. I'm waiting because I don't have enough information yet, and I deserve to make this decision from something better than a panic response. Her sister was quiet for a moment. Then she said: That sounds like something a therapist taught you. It was. And it was also, slowly, becoming something Claire knew herself.

Looking Ahead

The next chapter turns to a different but related question: not what you should do about this relationship, but what you need to understand about how the affair happened in the first place. That understanding does not excuse the betrayal. But it does something important, it makes it legible. And when harm becomes legible, it becomes possible to make decisions in light of what is true rather than in the fog of what remains unknown.

References

Amato, P. R. (2001). Children of divorce in the 1990s: An update of the Amato and Keith (1991) meta-analysis. *Journal of Family Psychology*, 15(3), 355–370. https://doi.org/10.1037/0893-3200.15.3.355

Gordon, K. C., Baucom, D. H., & Snyder, D. K. (2004). An integrative intervention for promoting recovery from extramarital affairs. *Journal of Marital and Family Therapy*,

30(2), 213–231. https://doi.org/10.1111/j.1752-0606.2004.tb01235.x

Gottman, J. M., & Silver, N. (1999). *The seven principles for making marriage work*. Crown Publishers.

Snyder, D. K., Castellani, A. M., & Whisman, M. A. (2006). Current status and future directions in couple therapy. *Annual Review of Psychology*, 57, 317–344. https://doi.org/10.1146/annurev.psych.56.091103.070154

Spring, J. A. (2012). *After the affair: Healing the pain and rebuilding trust when a partner has been unfaithful* (Rev. ed.). HarperCollins.

Willard, D. (2002). *Renovation of the heart: Putting on the character of Christ.* NavPress.

Chapter Six: Making It Legible: Understanding How the Affair Happened

"Not condemning does not mean condoning, and there is a world of difference between understanding and justifying."
— Esther Perel, The State of Affairs (2017)

Claire

In the weeks after Daniel confessed, Claire found herself returning to a single question. Not why did you do this, which she had asked many times, and not what were you thinking, which had produced answers she couldn't trust. The question that wouldn't leave her alone was simpler and stranger than either of those: Who are you?

She had been married to him for eleven years. She knew how he took his coffee. She knew the way he held his face when he was trying not to cry. She knew the name of the girl who had broken his heart in college and the particular grief he carried about his father, who had died without their relationship ever being repaired. She thought she knew him. And she had not known this.

The affair felt like more than a betrayal of trust. It felt like a revelation of someone she had never actually met. She wasn't sure which was worse: that he had deceived her, or that she was not sure anymore how much of what she had believed about their marriage had ever been real.

Evan

The question that would not leave Evan alone was not who are you. He knew who Amber was. He had lived with her for twenty-two years. He knew her laugh and her stubbornness and the particular way she shut down when she felt cornered. He knew her capacity for compartmentalization, he had always, in an abstract way, admired it, the ability to keep different aspects of life in separate boxes without apparent cost. He understood, now, what that capacity had been used for. His question was different. It was: how much of the last three years actually happened?

He meant this literally. The dinners that had been work events. The conferences she had attended. The late evenings she had explained with deadlines and demanding clients. He had been present for all of it, sitting across from her at dinner, lying next to her in bed, making decisions with her about the house and the finances and the summer plans, while a parallel life was occurring that he had not known about. The question of how the affair had happened was, for him, entangled with the question of whether the marriage he believed he had been living in had been real.

His therapist, whom he had started seeing in the fourth week, offered him a frame that helped, eventually. She said: the moments of genuine life in your marriage were real. The dinners that were dinners were real. The conversations that were what they appeared to be were real. The affair does not retroactively erase the real things. It adds something to them, a context you didn't know about but it doesn't unmake them.

He sat with that for a long time. He was not sure he fully believed it yet. But he held onto it, the way you hold onto something in the dark: not because you can see it, but because it is there.

* * *

Claire's disorientation is not unusual. It is, in fact, one of the defining features of betrayal trauma: the discovery doesn't only wound, it disorients. The person you trusted has turned out to be capable of something you would not have predicted. The history you shared has been retroactively altered. And the question that rises in that confusion — how could this have happened? — is not just an expression of pain. It is a genuine question.

This chapter addresses that question. Not in order to excuse the affair or redistribute responsibility for it, but because understanding how affairs develop is one of the most important tools a betrayed partner has. It reduces the disorientation. It makes the harm legible. And when harm becomes legible, decision-making becomes cleaner and less dependent on incomplete information.

Understanding is not the same as forgiving. It is not the same as reconciling. It does not require you to feel compassion for the person who hurt you, or to minimize what was done, or to take any specific next step in your relationship. It simply means you have a working map of what happened. Most people in the acute phase of betrayal are navigating without one.

Understanding is not the same as forgiving. It simply means you have a working map of what happened.

Affairs Do Not Happen All at Once

One of the most persistent myths about infidelity is that it erupts suddenly, that an otherwise faithful person is ambushed by circumstances and makes a single catastrophic choice. Occasionally that is true. More often it is not.

Shirley Glass, whose research on infidelity over three decades remains among the most carefully observed in the field, described the typical affair as emerging through a process of gradual boundary erosion rather than a single dramatic breach (Glass, 2003). The unfaithful partner does not usually wake up one morning and decide to betray their spouse. What happens, in most cases, is a series of small steps, each of which seems individually justifiable, that collectively move the person from one relational territory into another.

Glass identified a dynamic she called the walls-and-windows model. In a healthy primary relationship, transparency and emotional openness, what she called windows, face inward, toward the partner. The walls, the protective boundaries that guard against inappropriate intimacy with others, face outward. In the months before an affair, and often during it, that architecture gets quietly reversed: windows begin to open toward the affair partner, letting in emotional disclosure, vulnerability, and connection, while walls begin to rise against the primary partner, blocking them from the developing intimacy.

By the time many betrayed partners discover what has happened, this reversal is well underway. The unfaithful partner may feel, paradoxically, more understood by the affair partner than by their spouse, because that is where the emotional exchange has been occurring. The primary relationship, by contrast, has been getting a progressively managed, walled-off version of the person who lives within it.

This dynamic explains something that many betrayed partners find bewildering: why their spouse seemed to be present throughout the affair, not obviously distant, not visibly guilty, sometimes even warmer or more attentive than usual. The answer is that the architecture Glass describes does not always produce visible signs of distance. Some people, especially those who have learned to manage emotional disclosures carefully, can maintain the external forms of intimate relationship while the interior has shifted. The walls are high and invisible.

Why It Happened: What the Research Suggests

Researchers have studied infidelity from multiple angles and disciplines, and the honest summary is that no single explanation covers all cases. Affairs happen for different reasons in different relationships, and sometimes for several reasons at once. What the research does show is a cluster of contributing factors that appear repeatedly, across different studies and methodologies, and that are worth understanding.

Individual Factors

Some predispositions toward infidelity appear to be individual rather than relational. Research has consistently found that attachment insecurity particularly the anxious-attachment profile characterized by fear of abandonment and hypervigilance toward perceived rejection, and the avoidant profile characterized by discomfort with closeness and difficulty depending on others is associated with increased infidelity risk (Russell, Baker, & McNulty, 2013). This does not mean that every anxiously or avoidantly attached person will be unfaithful, nor that securely attached people are immune to affairs. It means that the specific relationship a person has with intimacy and dependency shapes how they respond when a primary relationship becomes difficult or unsatisfying.

Sexual attitudes shaped in the family of origin also play a documented role. Research on family-of-origin effects suggests that individuals who observed permissive attitudes toward infidelity in their families of origin, or who witnessed parental infidelity, carry a somewhat elevated statistical risk of being unfaithful themselves (Fife, Weeks, & Gambescia, 2020). This is not a deterministic claim. Plenty of people who grew up in families where infidelity was normalized choose a different path entirely, often because the harm they witnessed made them more committed to fidelity, not less. But it does indicate that the modeling we absorb about what relationships can and cannot bear leaves an impression.

Personality factors, including narcissistic traits and reduced capacity for empathy, have also been associated with infidelity in some research (Jonason et al., 2012). People who struggle to sustain empathic attunement to a partner's inner life, or who tend to organize their relational choices primarily around self-interest, are somewhat more likely to engage in behaviors that prioritize their own gratification at the partner's expense. This does not mean every unfaithful partner is a narcissist, most are not. But it does mean that the capacity to hold a partner's wellbeing in mind is not equally distributed, and that gaps in that capacity are relevant to understanding what happened.

Relational Factors

Affairs frequently, though not always, occur in the context of relational distress. Research by Hackathorn and Ashdown (2020) on the motivations people give for infidelity found that unmet emotional needs, including feeling unappreciated, emotionally disconnected, or chronically misunderstood are among the most commonly reported explanations unfaithful partners give for their choices.

It is important to hold this finding carefully. Unmet relational needs are not a justification for betrayal. Many people live for years with real relational loneliness and never become unfaithful. What the research points to is not a causal chain from relationship dissatisfaction to infidelity, but a contributing context that, when it interacts with individual vulnerabilities, opportunity, and a progressive lowering of internal constraints, increases risk.

This has a specific meaning for the betrayed partner. If your relationship had real difficulties before the affair, that does not mean you caused the affair, or that your partner's unfaithfulness was a proportionate or understandable response to those difficulties. It means the affair happened in a particular relational context, and that context may be part of what your partner needs to acknowledge and address as part of genuine accountability. Difficulty in a relationship is something both partners can explore together. Choosing deception is a unilateral act.

Difficulty in a relationship is something both partners can explore together. Choosing deception is a unilateral act.

Situational Factors

Situation and opportunity matter more than most people expect. Research by Munsch and Yorks (2018) examined infidelity rates across occupational contexts and found that both gender and occupational power dynamics shape the risk landscape in ways that are not primarily about character or relationship quality. Environments with high degrees of gender integration in positions of unequal authority, workplaces where individuals spend extended time with close colleagues of the opposite sex under conditions that produce shared stress and mutual dependence, and contexts where there is an ambient sense of being beyond normal accountability all contribute to elevated infidelity risk.

This finding does not excuse the affair. It contextualizes it. If your partner's affair involved a colleague, or developed in a professional context with these features, understanding that dynamic does not redistribute moral responsibility. But it does help explain how someone who was not consciously seeking an affair arrived at one. The opportunity and the context did not cause the infidelity, but they created conditions in which the internal brakes that would ordinarily have held were eroded.

When You Ask Your Partner Why

Many betrayed partners report that when they ask why, they receive answers that feel inadequate: I was unhappy. I don't know. It just happened. These responses are often experienced as further minimization. Sometimes they are. But research on how people understand their own motives, particularly in retrospect, suggests that unfaithful partners frequently lack the self-awareness to give a fully honest or accurate account of their own motivations at the time the affair occurred.

This does not excuse the inadequate explanation. Part of honest accountability is doing the internal work required to give a truthful and substantive answer, even if that takes time and therapeutic support. A partner committed to repair will work to understand their own motivations, not simply offer an explanation that minimizes discomfort or deflects responsibility.

If your partner's explanation for the affair still feels thin or incomplete, that instinct deserves attention. You are entitled to a real answer, not a packaged one.

The Role of Compartmentalization

One of the features of the affair experience that betrayed partners find hardest to accept is not the infidelity itself but the competence of the concealment. How did my partner manage to maintain this double life? How did they sit across the table from me, sleep beside me, attend our children's events, and carry this? Does the ease of the deception mean they feel nothing? Does it mean our relationship meant less to them than I believed?

The answer to these questions is psychological rather than moral, though the moral dimension is real. The capacity for compartmentalization, the ability to hold two incompatible emotional and behavioral realities in separate mental containers without allowing them to contaminate each other, is not equally distributed, but it is more widely available than most people realize. Some individuals can maintain a high degree of functional normalcy in one domain while engaging in behaviors that would be devastating to those who depend on them in another domain.

Research on self-deception and motivated reasoning is relevant here. People are remarkably capable of constructing internal narratives that reduce the psychological cost of their own choices (Trivers, 2011). An unfaithful partner may tell themselves that they are not really hurting their spouse if the spouse doesn't know. They may construct a narrative in which their unmet needs justify the search for satisfaction elsewhere. They may describe the affair partner as simply a friend, long after the relationship has become something else. These are not primarily conscious lies. They are the products of a motivated cognitive system that protects the person from the full weight of what they are doing.

Understanding this does not require you to feel compassion for it. But it does help explain why someone you know to be capable of genuine love and care could have sustained a deception that, from the outside, seems impossible to reconcile with that capacity.

What This Does Not Explain

After exploring these factors, it is important to be equally honest about what they do not explain or justify.

They do not explain why your partner chose betrayal rather than the alternatives available to them: an honest conversation about dissatisfaction, a request for couples therapy, a declaration that the marriage was in serious trouble. Even if every contributing factor described above was present, your partner had other options. The choice of deception over transparency is not explained by attachment style or occupational context or relational unhappiness. It is a choice, made by a person who had the capacity to choose otherwise.

They do not explain ongoing patterns of deception, trickle-truth disclosure, minimization of harm, or continued contact with the affair partner after discovery. Those behaviors, which are common in the acute phase of discovery, are not explained by the psychological dynamics that made the affair possible. They reflect a different set of choices being made in real time.

And they do not assign any portion of the moral weight of the betrayal to you. Relational difficulties are shared. The choice to respond to those difficulties with deception is not.

Relational difficulties are shared. The choice to respond to those difficulties with deception is not.

What a Genuine Accounting Looks Like

Researchers who study affair recovery have identified a specific kind of disclosure and accounting that is associated with better outcomes for the betrayed spouse. It is not simply more information, though information matters. It is a quality of accountability that demonstrates the unfaithful partner has honestly reckoned with what they did and why.

Snyder, Baucom, and Gordon's (2007) treatment model for affair recovery describes what they call a trauma-informed disclosure process, in which the unfaithful partner works toward a full and honest account of the affair that goes beyond the surface facts to include an honest exploration of their own motivations, vulnerabilities, and the ways they progressively set aside their awareness of harm. That kind of accounting is not natural or easy. It requires the unfaithful partner to hold in mind, for a sustained period, the full weight of what they did and how they did it, without retreating into self-justification or self-pity.

The practical markers of such an accounting are not complicated. The unfaithful partner demonstrates: an understanding of how the affair developed step by step, not just what happened at the end; an honest account of the choices they made along the way and the reasoning they used to justify them at the time; an acknowledgment that their partner's pain is proportionate to the harm, not excessive or unreasonable; and a willingness to answer follow-up questions without defensiveness, even if those questions are repeated, even if they are the same questions they have answered before.

If your partner is offering something less than this, it does not necessarily mean they are incapable of offering more. It may mean they have not yet done the work required to get there, or that they are managing shame in ways that prevent full transparency. Honest shame about harm caused is understandable. Managed shame that produces continued minimization or deflection is a problem that will need to be addressed if real repair is to occur.

Factors That Protect Against Future Infidelity

Understanding why the affair happened is one part of making sense of the situation. Understanding what conditions make future fidelity more likely is another, and one that matters regardless of whether the couple decides to stay together. A person who has experienced infidelity in one relationship, whether they stay in it or eventually leave, deserves to understand what protective conditions look like.

Research by Fye and Mims (2019) on protective factors against infidelity identified several conditions associated with reduced likelihood of affair behavior. These include: a strong personal commitment to fidelity as a value, rather than simply a behavioral compliance with expectation; clear and maintained boundaries around opposite-sex friendships, particularly in the context of emotional intimacy; transparent communication patterns within the primary relationship, especially around dissatisfaction; and active rather than passive investment in the relationship's quality.

What is notable about this list is that most of these are behavioral and relational conditions that can be developed, strengthened, or established even in people who do not initially possess them. They are not fixed personality traits. A person who has been unfaithful and is committed to change can work, with appropriate support, to establish the internal and relational architecture that makes future fidelity more likely.

For the betrayed partner, these factors are relevant in a different way. They provide a framework for evaluating whether the work your partner is doing, and the changes they are demonstrating, are the kind of work and change that matter for long-term trust. Vague reassurance, promises to try harder, and declarations of love are not structural changes. Movement toward real transparency, clear boundaries, and active investment in the relationship's repair is a different and more substantive category.

What This Means for Where You Are

You may be reading this chapter having already decided to leave the relationship. You may be reading it still in the early weeks of shock, with no decision made at all. You may be reading it having decided to stay and work toward repair. Whatever your situation, the understanding this chapter offers is not intended to change your direction. It is intended to give you a clearer picture of what you are working with.

For Those Who Are Staying

If you are in active repair with a partner who is engaged in real accountability, this chapter gives you a framework for evaluating the quality of that accountability. A partner who can articulate how the affair developed, who demonstrates real understanding of the harm they caused, and who is making structural changes rather than offering reassurances is giving you something real to work with. A partner who is still explaining rather than accounting, still managing disclosure rather than providing transparency, or still focused primarily on their own discomfort is not yet doing the work that repair requires.

For Those Who Are Leaving

If you have decided to leave, understanding how the affair happened is not primarily about the relationship you are exiting. It is about your own future. The patterns this chapter describes, attachment vulnerabilities, relational boundary erosion, situational opportunity combined with inadequate internal constraints are things that can develop in any intimate relationship. Understanding them helps you recognize them if they begin to develop in a future relationship, whether in your own behavior or in a future partner's.

For Those Who Are Still Waiting

If you are still in the deliberate-waiting position described in the previous chapter, this framework is a tool for gathering the information you need. What account is your partner giving of why the affair happened? Is that account honest and substantive, or managed and minimizing? Does it demonstrate honest self-understanding, or does it reflect the kind of motivated reasoning that makes affairs possible in the first place? These are not rhetorical questions. They are diagnostic ones. The quality of your partner's accounting is one of the most important sources of information available to you about whether genuine repair is possible.

A Reflection on Understanding and Judgment

For readers who carry a faith perspective into this process, the chapter's subject, understanding why the affair happened raises a specific challenge. Most faith traditions include a strong ethic of accountability. Wrongdoing is real, its consequences are real, and the person who caused harm bears full responsibility for it. That framework is not wrong, and this chapter is not asking you to set it aside.

But understanding how something happened is not the same as excusing it, and a faith perspective that refuses to engage with explanation because explanation feels like excuse has lost something important. The psalms of lament in the Hebrew scriptures do not simply condemn wrongdoing in the abstract. They sit with it. They ask God to account for the reality of evil and betrayal in the world with full seriousness. Lament assumes that harm is real, that it has a cause, and that the cause deserves to be examined, not because that examination will diminish the harm but because it will clarify it.

Willard describes the hardness of heart that precedes and enables serious betrayal as a spiritual condition that develops gradually, through a series of small choices that over time diminish the person's capacity to feel the full weight of what they are doing to those around them (Willard, 2002). The progressive boundary erosion that Glass documents is, in Willard's terms, also a spiritual erosion, a progressive withdrawal from the kind of interior transparency that genuine love requires.

This framework does not excuse the person who has become hard of heart. It explains the process by which ordinary people arrive at serious wrongdoing, and in doing so, it makes real repentance more rather than less possible. You cannot repent of something you have not accurately understood. And a faith community that insists on accountability without supporting honest understanding of how wrongdoing happened is demanding repentance without providing the self-knowledge that makes repentance real.

If your partner is willing to do the work this chapter describes, a faith perspective gives that work its full gravity and resource. The concept of honest confession, in the full theological sense, includes not only acknowledgment of what was done but honest reckoning with how and why. That kind of accounting is both psychologically and spiritually serious, and when it is done with integrity, it has the potential to change not just behavior but character.

For now, the task is simpler: to understand, as clearly as possible, what happened and why. That clarity is a gift you give yourself, regardless of what you decide to do with it.

* * *

Claire

It took several months of intensive work, including individual therapy for both of them and couples work with a specialist, before Claire began to get a full picture of how the affair had developed. Daniel's account had arrived in pieces, some of it volunteered, more of it drawn out by direct questions she learned to ask with increasing precision.

What she came to understand was this: the affair had not been the act of a man who had stopped loving her or who had secretly been a different person all along. It had been the act of a man who had accumulated, over a period of years, a set of unspoken needs and unexpressed dissatisfactions, who had not known how to bring those things into the relationship directly, who had encountered a context where intimacy was easy and consequence felt distant, and who had told himself a series of small lies that added up to something she still struggled to comprehend.

None of that made what he had done acceptable. It did not reduce her grief or the work still ahead of them.

But it made it legible. And in the strange grammar of healing, legibility turned out to be its own form of relief. She was not living in a marriage that had been fundamentally false. She was living in the aftermath of a failure she could now see clearly enough to understand. That was not the same as being over it. It was the beginning of knowing where she stood.

* * *

The next chapter turns from understanding to accountability. If you are staying, or considering it, the question becomes: what does real repair require from the person who caused this harm? Not reassurance, not a recalibrated version of the same relationship. Something harder and more specific than either of those. The Gottman framework's first phase, Atone, begins there.

Looking Ahead

Understanding how the affair happened is not the same as knowing what to do about it. The chapter ahead turns from comprehension to accountability, from the question of how we got here to the question of what honest repair actually looks like. If you are in a relationship where your partner is willing to do the work, Chapter Seven describes what that work consists of in concrete, behavioral terms: not what remorse sounds like, but what atonement does. And if you are not yet sure whether your partner is doing real work or performing it, that chapter offers the clearest framework available for telling the difference.

References

Fife, S. T., Weeks, G. R., & Gambescia, N. (2020). Family-of-origin and sexual attitudes and perceptions of infidelity. *Journal of Family Psychotherapy*, 31(1), 1–16. https://doi.org/10.1080/08975353.2020.1731498

Fye, M. A., & Mims, G. A. (2019). Preventing infidelity: A theory of protective factors. *The Family Journal*, 27(1), 22–30.

Glass, S. P. (2003). *Not 'just friends': Rebuilding trust and recovering your sanity after infidelity*. Free Press.

Gottman, J. M., & Silver, N. (2012). *What makes love last? How to build trust and avoid betrayal.* Simon & Schuster.

Hackathorn, J., & Ashdown, B. K. (2020). The lure of infidelity and costs to commitment: Motivational factors associated with infidelity. *Journal of Relationships Research*, 11, e11. https://doi.org/10.1017/jrr.2020.9

Jonason, P. K., Luevano, V. X., & Adams, H. M. (2012). How the dark triad traits predict relationship choices. *Personality and Individual Differences*, 53(3), 180–184. https://doi.org/10.1016/j.paid.2012.03.007

Munsch, C. L., & Yorks, T. P. (2018). When opportunity knocks: Who answers? Infidelity, gender, race, and occupational context. *Personal Relationships*, 25(4), 441–461. https://doi.org/10.1111/pere.12250

Perel, E. (2017). *The state of affairs: Rethinking infidelity*. Harper.

Russell, V. M., Baker, L. R., & McNulty, J. K. (2013). Attachment insecurity and infidelity in marriage: Do studies of dating relationships really inform us about marriage? *Journal of Family Psychology*, 27(2), 242–251. https://doi.org/10.1037/a0032118

Snyder, D. K., Baucom, D. H., & Gordon, K. C. (2007). *Getting past the affair: A program to help you cope, heal, and move on—together or apart.* Guilford Press.

Trivers, R. (2011). *The folly of fools: The logic of deceit and self-deception in human life.* Basic Books.

Willard, D. (2002). *Renovation of the heart: Putting on the character of Christ.* NavPress.

Part 3: What Repair Requires

Chapter Seven: What Repair Actually Requires: The Work of Atonement

"Genuine contrition is not a feeling. It is a direction."
— paraphrase of Dallas Willard, Renovation of the Heart

Claire

Three months after Daniel confessed, Claire's therapist asked her a question she had not been asked before: "Not what he said. What did he do?"

Claire sat with that for a long time. He had apologized. He had cried. He had said he was sorry more times than she could count, in language that sounded, most days, like it meant something. But when she moved past the words and tried to answer the actual question, what he had done, the list was shorter than she expected. He had answered some of her questions. He had agreed to come to therapy. He had, as far as she could tell, stopped contact with the other woman.

But he had not opened his phone to her without being asked. He had not told her the full story without needing to be pressed, question by careful question. He had not explained, on his own initiative, what had happened to their finances during the affair. He had not asked her what she needed. He had apologized, but he had not atoned.

Her therapist gently named the difference. "Remorse is what you feel. Atonement is what you do. One lives in the heart. The other lives in behavior, over time."

Evan

Evan asked himself the same question. Not what had Amber said. What had she done.

She had wept, when he confronted her. She had said she was sorry more times than he could track. She had made gestures he recognized as sincere in their feeling, if incomplete in their effect: she had initiated conversations about the future of the marriage, she had agreed to couples therapy, she had said, several times, that she would do whatever it took. In the weeks after discovery, she had been, to all observable appearances, remorseful.

But she had not opened her phone to him. She had answered his specific questions without volunteering anything beyond the minimum. When he asked whether there was anything else he did not know, she said: No. When he pushed, there are things I'm not asking the right questions to ask, and I need to know whether there are things I'm not asking, she had said: I've told you everything. And the following month, a detail had emerged that contradicted something she had told him in month one. Not a large thing. But a thing.

He understood the difference, by that point, between remorse and accountability. Remorse was something Amber had. He could see it in her, and he did not doubt it. But accountability, the complete account, the full story, the willingness to hand him the information he needed to understand his own life, that, she was not yet providing. And without it, the remorse floated free of any real foundation. You could not build on regret. You could only build on truth.

He came to this understanding slowly, over the course of several months, through conversations with his therapist and through the particular education of watching the gap between what Amber said and what she did. By the time he could name it clearly, he had also begun to understand something harder: that he could not produce the accountability she was not yet willing to offer. He could ask. He had asked. What happened after the asking was not under his control.

* * *

If you are reading this chapter, you are likely somewhere in the terrain that Claire was navigating: the territory between initial disclosure and real repair. You may have received apologies. You may have heard your partner say they are sorry, that they never meant to hurt you, that they understand what they did. And some part of you may still be waiting for something you cannot quite name. What you are waiting for is probably atonement. Not just the word, but the work.

This chapter is about what that work actually looks like. It draws on the Gottman framework's first phase of affair recovery, what John and Julie Gottman call the Atone phase, and places it in conversation with what research and clinical observation have documented about the conditions that make real trust repair possible. It is written primarily for the betrayed spouse, but it is equally relevant if you are trying to evaluate whether what your partner is offering constitutes real repair or a performance of it.

The distinction matters enormously. A partner who is performing repair, who is managing their image, minimizing damage, and hoping you will eventually feel better without being required to do much will produce a very different trajectory than a partner who is actually doing the work. Learning to tell the difference is one of the most important things you can do right now.

Remorse and Atonement: Why They Are Not the Same Thing

Remorse is an emotional state. It refers to the feeling of guilt, regret, or sorrow that follows a recognized wrong. Many unfaithful partners experience real remorse. They feel bad about what they did. They carry guilt. They wish it had not happened. These are real feelings, and when they are authentic they matter.

But remorse is not the same as atonement, and confusing the two is one of the most common sources of stalled recovery in the aftermath of an affair.

Atonement, in its most direct meaning, is the process of making right. It involves acknowledgment of harm, honest reckoning with the weight of what was done, and sustained behavioral change that demonstrates the accountability is real rather than rhetorical. It is not a single event but an ongoing posture. And it is not primarily about the unfaithful partner's internal experience of guilt. It is about what happens for the person who was harmed.

"Remorse lives in the heart. Atonement lives in behavior, sustained over time."

Researchers who study forgiveness and relational repair have found that what betrayed partners most need is not simply to know that their partner feels bad but to receive evidence, through consistent behavior, that the partner understands the gravity of what they did and has made an actual internal commitment to being different (Gordon, Baucom, & Snyder, 2004). The feeling of remorse, without that evidence, can feel less like comfort and more like another form of self-involvement on the part of the person who caused the harm.

This is why many betrayed spouses report feeling strangely unmoved by an unfaithful partner's tears or visible suffering. It is not callousness. It is an accurate reading of the situation. Suffering is not the same as repair. Feeling bad is not the same as becoming trustworthy. And the nervous system of a betrayed spouse, wired by trauma to monitor safety rather than sentiment, is often exquisitely sensitive to the difference.

What the Gottman Approach Calls for in the Atone Phase

John and Julie Gottman, drawing substantially on the late Peggy Vaughan's survey research on affair recovery outcomes, identified the Atone phase as the indispensable foundation of their three-stage model. Vaughan studied couples in which an affair had been disclosed and tracked which relationships survived and which did not. Her findings, which has been corroborated by subsequent research, was striking: couples who talked thoroughly and honestly about the affair, with the unfaithful partner answering questions with transparency and expressing real remorse, were far more likely to stay together and to report recovery (Vaughan, 2002).

Couples who tried to skip this phase, who agreed to move on without fully processing what had happened tended to cycle through repeated crises without progressing through them.

The Gottmans identified four central goals for this phase of treatment. Each of them is worth examining not as a clinical protocol but as a description of what real repair requires.

Goal One: The Expression of Real Remorse

The first goal is facilitating a real expression of remorse from the unfaithful partner. Not a rehearsed apology. Not a minimizing summary. Remorse that acknowledges the particular harm done to the specific person sitting across from them.

This sounds simple. It is rarely simple. Many unfaithful partners find real remorse difficult to sustain, for reasons that vary. Some are defended against it by shame, shame operates differently from guilt, and where guilt says I did something wrong, shame says I am fundamentally bad, a distinction that matters because shame tends to produce withdrawal and self-protection rather than movement toward the person who was harmed. Others are defended by their own unresolved emotional needs: the desire to be understood, or the lingering attachment to the affair partner, or the ongoing use of rationalizations that soften the weight of what was done. Still others are frightened by the depth of the betrayed partner's pain and respond to it with minimization, emotional shutdown, or a premature push toward resolution because their own discomfort with the pain is intolerable.

None of these responses are adequate. And when you encounter them, when the apology feels hollow, when the remorse seems to have a time limit, when your partner grows frustrated with how long your pain is lasting, you are not being unreasonable. You are recognizing that the repair process has stalled before it has begun.

When Remorse Is Real, and When It Is Not

Real remorse tends to have certain recognizable qualities. It acknowledges the particular harm done, not just the general outcome. It does not seek to explain the affair in ways that distribute responsibility to the betrayed partner. It tolerates repeated expressions of pain without growing impatient or defensive. It leads to behavioral change, not just verbal expression.

Remorse that is primarily performative tends to look different. It may be intense at first but fades quickly once the initial crisis passes. It often comes with minimizing language: at least it was only…, it wasn't as serious as you think, or we can put this behind us now. It may seek reassurance from the betrayed partner rather than offering comfort. And it tends to redirect conversation toward the unfaithful partner's experience of guilt rather than staying focused on the betrayed partner's experience of harm. You are entitled to notice this difference. You are also entitled to name it clearly.

Goal Two: Transparency—The Foundation of New Trust

The second goal of the Atone phase is establishing full transparency. The Gottmans describe this with striking directness: only honesty will heal the prior deceptions and begin to re-establish trust.

What this means in practice is that the unfaithful partner makes an active, consistent commitment to openness that is not contingent on being asked. This is a critical distinction. Transparency that only arrives in response to direct questions is not transparency. It is selective disclosure, a more limited version of the same information management that characterized the affair itself.

Full transparency means the unfaithful partner volunteers relevant information rather than waiting to be caught. It means they answer questions completely and without defensive hedging. It means access to communications, whereabouts, and accounts is freely offered rather than grudgingly negotiated. It means that when something happens that is relevant to the betrayed partner's sense of safety, an unexpected message from the affair partner, an unanticipated contact, anything that the betrayed partner would want to know, it is disclosed proactively, not concealed until discovered.

The reason transparency matters so much is not primarily practical, though the practical dimension is real. It matters because the affair itself was sustained by a systematic reversal of openness in the marriage: the unfaithful partner's interior life, their whereabouts, their communications, their developing emotional connection elsewhere, all of it was walled off from the person they were supposed to be most open with. Shirley Glass described this as the reversal of walls and windows: in a healthy primary relationship, openness faces inward, toward the partner, while protective boundaries face outward. An affair requires, and sustains, the opposite architecture (Glass, 2003).

Full transparency is the architectural repair. It does not just provide information. It begins to reconstruct the relational structure that the affair dismantled.

Transparency that only arrives in response to questions is not transparency. It is the same information management that sustained the affair.

Transparency has limits, and those limits deserve equal attention. It does not require the betrayed spouse to have unlimited access to every communication their partner has ever had with anyone. It does not require confession of every past detail of the affair, particularly graphic details of sexual activity, which research consistently shows produces intrusive imagery that worsens rather than relieves traumatic symptoms (Gottman & Gottman, 2017). And it does not require an atmosphere of surveillance and interrogation that, over time, degrades the relationship rather than rebuilding it.

What it requires is a real shift in posture: from information management to radical openness, as a consistent practice, sustained not because it is demanded but because it is understood to be necessary for the rebuilding of a relationship in which trust is possible.

Goal Three: Verification and the Work of Becoming Credible

Trust that has been broken cannot simply be declared restored. It has to be rebuilt incrementally, through a process of consistent behavior observed over time (Gottman & Silver, 2012). The Gottman framework names this as a central goal of the Atone phase: creating conditions in which the unfaithful partner's trustworthiness is not merely asserted but verified.

For many betrayed spouses, this involves a period in which they check. They look at the phone. They ask for location confirmations. They follow up on stated plans. They notice discrepancies between what was said and what was found. This behavior, which is frequently pathologized as "snooping" or characterized as obsessive by the unfaithful partner, is in fact a rational response to an information environment that has been demonstrated to be unreliable. It is hypervigilance in the service of safety, which is exactly what the nervous system does after a major breach of trust.

A partner who is committed to repair will understand this and respond to it with patience rather than resentment. They will not only tolerate the checking; they will actively support it. They will understand that the hypervigilance is not a character defect in the betrayed spouse but a reasonable response to having been systematically deceived, and that the only path through it is for their own behavior to become reliably trustworthy over a sustained period.

This takes time. Research on trust repair in the aftermath of betrayal suggests that consistent trustworthy behavior needs to be observed across different contexts, over an extended period, before the nervous system of a betrayed partner begins to relax its vigilance (Gottman, 2011; Snyder, Baucom, & Gordon, 2007). There are no shortcuts. A partner who becomes frustrated with how long the process takes, or who interprets the checking as an accusation, is signaling that they do not yet understand what their behavior cost and what it requires to rebuild.

Goal Four: Hearing the Pain Without Shutting It Down

The fourth goal of the Atone phase is perhaps the most demanding: the unfaithful partner must be available to the betrayed partner's pain. Not available in the sense of tolerating brief expressions of upset before redirecting the conversation. Available in the sense of being present, patient, and non-defensive while the person they harmed articulates the full weight of that harm, including emotions that are difficult to receive.

This matters in ways that are easy to underestimate. The research on affair recovery consistently identifies the quality of the unfaithful partner's listening, their ability to hear the betrayed partner's experience without becoming defensive, minimizing, or counterattacking, as one of the strongest predictors of recovery outcome (Gottman & Gottman, 2017). It is not the apology that does the most work. It is the quality of the witness.

What good listening looks like in this context is concrete. It means hearing expressions of anger without treating them as attacks. It means allowing the betrayed partner to ask the same question more than once without signaling impatience, because repeated questions in the wake of betrayal are not obstinacy, they are the nervous system's effort to fully process what happened. It means saying I understand how you would feel that way, and meaning it, even when it is hard to hear. It means resisting the impulse to explain, to contextualize, to defend, or to prematurely move toward resolution when the betrayed partner is not yet ready for any of those things.

The Gottmans are specific about one important limit here. The betrayed partner can be gently redirected, with care and empathy, away from questions about the explicit sexual details of the affair. This is not because those questions are unreasonable, they are entirely understandable but because the answers tend to produce intrusive visual imagery that amplifies rather than soothes traumatic symptoms. The goal of the disclosure conversation is not comprehensive coverage of every detail but enough honesty and accountability to begin establishing the betrayed partner's sense of having been told the truth.

The Concrete Behaviors of Real Repair

Abstract language about accountability and remorse is easy to produce. Behavioral change is harder, and it is the concrete change that matters. The following is not a checklist but a description of the behaviors that research and clinical observation have identified as meaningful markers of atonement.

Telling the Full Story, Once

Full disclosure is not a pleasant conversation. It is among the hardest things an unfaithful partner will do. It requires giving an honest account of what happened: when the affair began, how long it lasted, the nature of the relationship with the affair partner, and whether contact has now ended. It does not require graphic sexual detail, but it does require honest answers to the factual questions that shape the betrayed partner's understanding of their own life.

Research on outcomes in affair recovery indicates that incremental disclosure, what clinicians often call trickle-truth, is considerably more damaging to the recovery process than full initial disclosure, even when the full story is painful (Snyder et al., 2007). When a betrayed spouse discovers additional information after having been told the story was complete, the breach of trust is re-activated. They are not simply dealing with the original affair. They are dealing with the ongoing deception that surrounded it, and that deception often feels, to many betrayed spouses, like its own separate and serious harm.

A partner who is committed to repair will tell the story fully, not in pieces, not with omissions they are hoping will remain undiscovered. This is not primarily a moral demand, though the moral dimension is real. It is a practical necessity for the recovery process to have any integrity.

A Note for the Reader Whose Partner Has Not Fully Disclosed

If you are not sure whether you have received the full story, trust that uncertainty. It is not paranoia. Betrayed spouses have an often accurate intuition that something is still missing, particularly when the disclosed account has gaps, when emotional details feel inconsistent, or when the account of the relationship's end seems too clean.

You have the right to ask directly: Is there anything else I do not know? Is there anything you have told me that is not fully accurate? You have the right to name clearly that trickle-truth has consequences, and that each new disclosure discovered rather than volunteered resets the process of trust repair considerably.

If your partner refuses to give you a full account or continues to offer incomplete and shifting versions of what happened, that is important information about what kind of repair is available to you. It does not tell you what to do. But it tells you something clear about where you stand.

Ending Contact, Completely and Transparently

If the affair is ongoing at the time of disclosure, or if contact with the affair partner has continued after disclosure, there is no repair process underway. There is crisis management, and sometimes image management, but real repair cannot begin in an environment where the breach of the relationship's boundaries is still occurring.

Complete ending of contact means exactly what it implies. It means no communication of any kind with the affair partner: not by text, not by email, not through mutual social networks, not the occasional check-in to "make sure they are okay." It means, where the affair partner is a workplace colleague, taking concrete steps to restructure professional arrangements to minimize unavoidable contact and fully disclosing any unavoidable interactions to the betrayed spouse. It means not maintaining a covert channel of communication under the rationalization that it is "just as friends" or that the affair partner deserves closure.

A partner who presents ending contact as too difficult, who argues that they have obligations to the affair partner, or who maintains a residual connection under any framing, is not yet in the Atone phase of recovery. They are in ambivalence, and the two should not be confused. Ambivalence is a real phenomenon that can be worked through with good therapeutic support. But it is not repair, and treating ambivalence as though it were repair, moving forward with the relationship while the attachment to the affair partner remains alive produces the cycling pattern of partial reconciliation followed by re-crisis that characterizes stalled recovery.

Complete ending of contact is not a demand that exceeds the limits of fair repair. It is the minimum precondition for any repair at all.

Patience With the Timeline

Healing from betrayal is not linear, and it is not fast. This is not a flaw in the process. It is what recovery from relational trauma looks like.

Many betrayed spouses report that they felt they were making progress, the acute flooding had begun to ease, they were sleeping somewhat better, the obsessive cycling of questions had quieted and then something triggered a full return to the acute phase: a song, an anniversary, a passing reference, a moment when their partner's phone buzzed and something tightened in their chest before they could stop it. These returns are not regression. They are the normal architecture of trauma recovery.

The Gottman framework notes that the Atone phase lasts as long as the betrayed partner needs it to. This is not imprecision. It is direct recognition that the length of the recovery process is not determined by the unfaithful partner's sense of how long is reasonable, but by the actual arc of healing in the person who was harmed. A partner who signals, through sighs, impatience, subtle withdrawal, or direct statements that the betrayed spouse's continued pain is a burden or an imposition is communicating something important about what their commitment to repair actually contains.

Patience is not passive waiting. It is active, sustained, compassionate presence. It means showing up in the same way on the difficult day six months from now as on the difficult day two weeks after discovery. It means not treating the healing process as having concluded simply because things have improved or because the unfaithful partner's own discomfort with the situation has resolved. Healing is the betrayed partner's journey, and real repair walks alongside that journey wherever it goes.

Why Atonement Is Not the Same as Punishment

Some readers may be uneasy with the demands this chapter describes. It can feel, from the outside, as though the Atone phase asks the unfaithful partner to submit indefinitely to punishment, to check-ins and scrutiny and the ongoing rehearsal of a past they are trying to move beyond.

Punishment is imposed from outside; atonement is chosen from within. Punishment seeks retribution; atonement seeks repair. Punishment has no necessary relationship to the restoration of trust; atonement is precisely oriented toward that restoration. And the key behavioral marker that separates them is whether the unfaithful partner is doing the work willingly, because they understand why it is necessary and are committed to what it aims to accomplish, or resentfully, because they feel coerced and are waiting for the requirement to end.

A partner who is truly atoning does not experience the transparency requirements as punishment. They understand why the hypervigilance exists. They understand that their own choices created the conditions that made constant verification necessary. They are willing to do what is required, whatever timeline is required, because they grasp the weight of what they did and are committed to becoming credibly trustworthy rather than simply appearing so.

When this willingness is present, the Atone phase, for all its difficulty, has a particular quality. There is a kind of relational seriousness in it that many couples in recovery describe, in retrospect, as having been unexpectedly meaningful, a radical honesty, an enforced attention to what the relationship was and what both people needed, that had not been present before. Willard (2002) described the willingness to submit to honest moral reckoning as a form of soul formation, not punishment, but the serious work of becoming a different kind of person. Atonement, when it is genuine, is not only relational. It is the work of character.

When the Unfaithful Partner Will Not Atone

Everything described so far assumes a partner who is willing to engage the repair process, even if imperfectly and with the stumbles that real effort involves. But not all unfaithful partners are willing. Some refuse the process entirely. Some engage it briefly, then withdraw when the sustained demands become clear. Some perform atonement while quietly maintaining the very patterns. secrecy, image management, selective disclosure that sustained the affair itself. This is among the hardest realities to face in the aftermath of betrayal, and it deserves to be named without flinching. If your partner has expressed remorse but is not doing the behavioral work of atonement, you are not in a repair process. You are in a holding pattern, waiting for repair that has not yet begun.

If your partner has responded to your questions with defensiveness, minimization, or anger, if they have treated your need for information as an attack, your hypervigilance as a character flaw, your slow healing as an act of hostility they are not currently in the Atone phase. They may be in shame, or fear, or ambivalence, or self-deception about what they owe. All of those can potentially be worked through, with time and good therapeutic support. But they are not repair, and waiting for them to become repair without any structural intervention is not a strategy.

The Gottmans are clear about the consequence of this reality: without real willingness to atone, including transparency, remorse, and behavioral accountability, the restoration of trust is not possible. This is not a moral judgment about the unfaithful partner's character. It is a description of what the process requires. A partner who is unwilling to provide what repair demands is, functionally, a partner who has chosen not to repair, whatever language they are using to describe their intentions.

If Your Partner Refuses the Atone Process: What You Can Do

Name what you observe, directly and specifically. Not as an accusation, but as a statement of fact: I have not received a complete account of what happened. I do not have access to the communications that are relevant to my sense of safety. When I express pain, I receive defensiveness rather than presence. State what you need, also precisely. Not what your partner should feel, but what you need from their behavior in order to have any basis for continuing to work on this relationship. Give the stated needs a fair opportunity to be met. Change takes time, and some partners need a clear statement of requirements before they understand what is being asked.

If, after a reasonable period, the behavior has not changed, allow that information to inform your decisions. You cannot repair a relationship alone. Continuing to invest in a process your partner is not engaged in is not commitment. It is a form of self-erasure.

Find individual support if you do not have it. The decision about what to do when a partner refuses repair is one of the most significant decisions you will make. It should not be made in isolation.

The Role of Faith in Atonement

For readers whose lives are shaped by faith, the language of this chapter will carry resonances that psychology cannot quite reach. Atonement, in its deepest sense, is a theological concept before it is a clinical one. It names a return, a movement of the self, back toward a moral home from which it has strayed, and back toward the relationship that was broken by that straying.

The Hebrew and Christian traditions carry rich resources for understanding this kind of return. The Hebrew word shub, translated in the Old Testament as "repentance," literally means to turn around, to reorient the direction of movement. It is not primarily about feeling bad. It is about going in a different direction. The New Testament's word metanoia carries similar freight: a change of mind that becomes a change of life.

For both traditions, repentance is not a one-time transaction but a sustained reorientation. It is not completed by an apology or even by a period of contrition. It is evidenced by a life that has been changed. Willard (2002), whose work on spiritual formation has shaped so much serious Christian thinking about character, understood this clearly: the goal of repentance is not the management of behavior but the transformation of the person who produced the behavior. That transformation takes time, requires grace, and cannot be performed or faked.

For the betrayed spouse in a faith context, this framing offers something valuable. It names the demand for atonement not as punitive but as spiritually serious, as the actual, costly work of becoming someone whose word can be trusted and whose relationship is built on honesty rather than managed appearances. It also names what the betrayed spouse is asked to hold: not cheap grace, which requires nothing and changes nothing, but the more demanding patience of waiting for evidence that the transformation is real.

Walter Brueggemann's (2002) work on lament is relevant here for a different reason. Lament is the tradition of taking grief and loss to God honestly, naming the magnitude of what has been broken rather than wrapping it in premature comfort. For the betrayed spouse who is also a person of faith, the pressure to forgive quickly, to move on for the sake of the marriage and the family, to find resolution in religious language that papers over anguish, can be one of the more subtle and damaging forms of spiritual bypass. Brueggemann's insistence that lament is a legitimate and necessary part of the faith life offers a different framework: your grief is not a failure of faith. It is an act of honesty before God, and it deserves to be honored rather than hurried.

The same God who calls the unfaithful partner to repentance accompanies the betrayed spouse through the long work of healing. That accompaniment does not erase the pain. It carries it.

* * *

Claire

Several months into the process, something shifted for Claire. Not a dramatic moment, not a clear threshold, but an accumulation.

Daniel had begun, finally, to do the work she had been waiting for. He had told her the full story without being pressed. He had offered the phone, the email, access to every communication she wanted, without framing it as a concession or a punishment. He had answered her questions, the same questions asked more than once from different angles, with patience she had not expected and did not entirely trust at first. When she wept, he did not try to stop it or redirect it toward reassurance. He sat with it.

She did not yet know whether the marriage would survive. She could not yet say whether the trust could ever be rebuilt to the degree she would need. Those questions were still open, and she had stopped trying to close them before she had the information they required.

But she knew something she had not known before, the person she was dealing with was no longer managing her. He was, for the first time since the discovery, there.

That was not reconciliation. It was not forgiveness. It was something smaller and, in its own way, more significant. It was the beginning of having something real to work with.

The chapters ahead will address what that work looks like when both partners are engaged in it: the attunement skills that begin to rebuild emotional connection, the conflict tools that address the underlying patterns that left the relationship vulnerable, and the long, careful work of reconstructing a shared life on different foundations. That work is real and it is possible, and it begins exactly here—with the willingness to stop performing repair and start doing it.

* * *

A Word to the Reader Who Is Doing This Alone

Not everyone reading this chapter has a partner who is willing to atone. Some of you are carrying the harm of betrayal in a relationship where your partner is still minimizing, still managing, still directing more energy toward protecting their image than toward your healing. Some of you have received partial disclosures and suspect there is more. Some of you have been told that your pain is the problem.

This chapter has been honest about what real repair requires because you deserve to know what it looks like. Not so that you can force it, it cannot be forced, but so that you can accurately assess what you are being offered, and make decisions about your own life on the basis of clear information rather than hope that is not yet grounded in evidence.

If you are not receiving what this chapter describes, that is important to know. It does not automatically mean you should leave.

People change, sometimes slowly and with much more resistance than we would wish, and the distance between a partner who is not yet atoning and one who is capable of repair is not always fixed. It may be closed through skilled therapeutic intervention, through time, through the clarity of a direct conversation in which you name what you need and what the consequences are if those needs are not met.

But it may not be. And your own healing does not have to wait for that determination. The stabilization work, the grief work, the slow rebuilding of your own sense of self and safety, that work belongs to you, and it can move forward regardless of what your partner chooses to do. You are not only the protagonist of this marriage. You are the protagonist of your own life.

The next chapter turns from the work of the unfaithful partner to the work of the couple together. The Attunement phase of the Gottman model addresses how two people who have been significantly damaged begin to rebuild their capacity to hear each other, to express needs without weaponizing them, and to manage conflict in ways that do not re-inflict the original harm. That work is harder and more reciprocal than the Atone phase. It also, for couples who are truly in it together, begins to contain something other than loss.

Looking Ahead

Accountability is the foundation. But a relationship cannot be rebuilt on a foundation alone. Once the full disclosure has been given, the contact has ended, and the behavior has begun to match the remorse, something else is required, something harder in some ways to produce than even an honest accounting of the harm done.

Chapter Eight addresses that next layer of work: what it means for two people to turn back toward each other emotionally, how that movement happens after a breach of trust this serious, and what it looks like when it is real rather than performed. The Atone phase makes repair possible. The Attune phase is where it begins to feel like something.

References

Brueggemann, W. (2002). *Spirituality of the Psalms.* Fortress Press.

Glass, S. P. (2003). *Not 'just friends': Rebuilding trust and recovering your sanity after infidelity.* Free Press.

Gordon, K. C., Baucom, D. H., & Snyder, D. K. (2004). An integrative intervention for promoting recovery from extramarital affairs. *Journal of Marital and Family Therapy,* 30(2), 213–231. https://doi.org/10.1111/j.1752-0606.2004.tb01235.x

Gottman, J. M. (2011). *The science of trust: Emotional attunement for couples.* W. W. Norton.

Gottman, J. M., & Gottman, J. S. (2017). *Treating affairs and trauma: A Gottman approach for therapists on the treatment of affairs and posttraumatic stress.* Gottman Institute.

Gottman, J. M., & Silver, N. (2012). *What makes love last? How to build trust and avoid betrayal.* Simon & Schuster.

Snyder, D. K., Baucom, D. H., & Gordon, K. C. (2007). *Getting past the affair: A program to help you cope, heal, and move on—together or apart.* Guilford Press.

Vaughan, P. (2002). *The monogamy myth: A personal handbook for recovering from affairs* (3rd ed.). Newmarket Press.

Willard, D. (2002). *Renovation of the heart: Putting on the character of Christ.* NavPress.

Chapter Eight: Attune: Rebuilding Emotional Connection

"What I needed was not for him to fix it. I needed to know he could feel it."

— composite, from a group conversation about repair

The Atone phase of recovery asks one thing of the unfaithful partner above all others: accountability. It asks for honesty, for the cessation of deception, for a willingness to answer questions and absorb pain without retreating into self-protection. That work is necessary and irreducible. Without it, nothing else is possible.

But accountability, even sincere accountability, is not the same as connection. A partner can offer a full disclosure, take responsibility for every specific act of harm, and still leave the betrayed spouse sitting in a room with someone they cannot quite reach. The relief of knowing the truth, however partial, does not automatically restore the sense of being known and cared for that betrayal destroyed. The path from honesty to intimacy is longer than it might appear, and it requires something that is harder in some ways to produce than even a clean disclosure: the capacity to be emotionally present to another person's pain without running from it.

That is what Attunement means in the Gottman framework. Not shared hobbies or well-managed conversations. Not the absence of conflict or the performance of happiness. Attunement is the capacity to turn toward a partner's emotional experience with interest and care, to feel enough of what they are feeling that they do not feel utterly alone in it, and to respond in ways that say: I see you, I am with you, and your inner life matters to me.

This chapter is about that work. It addresses the attunement skills that the Gottman research has identified as central to the rebuilding of a relationship after betrayal: bids for connection and how they function, the role of emotional responsiveness in trust repair, how to manage conflict without retraumatizing a partner who is already carrying elevated nervous system load, and what it looks like when two people are actually finding their way back toward each other rather than simply coexisting in a household. It also addresses what happens when this work is asymmetrical or absent, because for many couples, the capacity to attune has never been equally distributed, and the affair did not emerge in a relational vacuum.

None of this is easy. It requires that both partners be simultaneously wounded and working, grieving and building, honest about what was lost and open to something that is not yet fully formed. For many couples, the Attune phase is the one that strains them most, because it asks them to be present to each other before the wounds have healed, and in many cases before trust has been rebuilt to the point where presence feels safe. The reason to do it anyway is not optimism. It is that without it, repair remains a project being managed rather than a relationship being rebuilt.

What Attunement Is, and Why It Matters After Betrayal

The word attunement comes originally from music. To be in tune with someone is to be operating in the same key, to recognize when the notes you are producing harmonize or clash with the notes the other person is producing, and to adjust accordingly. In relational science, the concept carries similar meaning. Attunement is not simply listening. It is a kind of emotional tracking that allows one person to register the internal state of another and respond in ways that make the other person feel received rather than processed.

John Gottman's decades of research on what distinguishes couples who stay together from couples who do not led him to identify one of the most consistent predictors of long-term relationship health: the tendency to turn toward rather than away from a partner's bids for connection (Gottman & Silver, 2015; Gottman, 2011). A bid, in this research, is any attempt by one partner to make contact with the other. It can be obvious and direct: "I'm struggling today and I need to talk." It can be so subtle it barely registers: a sigh, a comment about the weather, a glance toward a partner that lingers half a second longer than ordinary. The content of the bid is often not its real content. The real content is a question underneath the surface: Are you there? Do you notice me? Am I still someone who matters to you?

Attunement is a kind of emotional tracking that allows one person to register the internal state of another and respond in ways that make the other person feel received rather than processed.

Couples who are emotionally healthy, even without knowing the term, answer yes to that question consistently. They turn toward bids at rates far higher than couples in distress. They do not turn toward every bid, and they do not respond to every moment of contact with full emotional engagement. But they have a default orientation of responsiveness, and their partner feels the weight of that orientation even in small, passing interactions (Gottman & Silver, 2015).

After betrayal, this entire architecture is disrupted. The betrayed spouse has discovered that the person they turned toward for safety was, for an extended period of time, not fully present. The attunement they experienced, or believed they experienced, during the affair period was occurring alongside a parallel, hidden life. This means that every remembered moment of apparent connection during the period of the affair is now potentially suspect. Was that tenderness real? Was that conversation real? When my partner seemed to be with me, were they elsewhere?

These questions are not paranoia. They are the reasonable response of a mind that has learned it cannot trust its own prior readings of the relationship. The hypervigilance that betrayed spouses experience is, in part, an attempt to solve this problem: if I monitor everything closely enough, I can detect the gap between what my partner presents and what is happening inside them. I will not be fooled again.

The problem is that hypervigilance is not a sustainable state, and it does not actually resolve the underlying wound. What the betrayed spouse needs, at some level they may not yet be able to fully articulate, is not just the absence of lies. It is the restoration of connection, the sense that when their partner looks at them, something real is passing between them. That sense cannot be faked, and it cannot be produced by the effort of either partner in isolation. It requires something that must be built between them. That is what the Attune phase is attempting to rebuild.

The ATTUNE Framework

Gottman (2011) formalizes this work in a six-component framework known as ATTUNE, a structured account of what emotionally available partners do when they are present to each other. The acronym is not a performance checklist. It is a description of an interior orientation made visible in behavior. Each component builds on the one before it, and together they describe not a skill set but a way of being turned toward another person.

A - Awareness

Awareness, in the Gottman sense, is the ongoing project of understanding what is happening in your partner's inner life: their current stresses, their emotional preoccupations, their fears and longings, the texture of where they are right now. For couples with a healthy emotional culture, this awareness is built through years of small conversations, accumulated knowledge about each other's patterns, and the general practice of paying attention. For couples navigating repair after betrayal, it must be rebuilt more deliberately.

For the unfaithful partner, awareness after betrayal means developing a particular attention to what the betrayed spouse is carrying. Not only the large grief that is visible, but the subtler expressions of it: the moment a song triggers something, the evening when ordinary tiredness has an edge to it that suggests more than fatigue, the morning when everything seems functional, but the eyes carry a distance. The Gottman research calls this maintaining a detailed mental map of a partner's inner world, and it is one of the consistent features of relationships that report high intimacy (Gottman & Silver, 2015).

This kind of attention cannot be simulated. Betrayed spouses, whose threat-detection systems have been calibrated by the experience of deception, are often acutely sensitive to the difference between a partner who is tracking their experience and a partner who is performing interest. The performance is, in its own way, another form of distance. What the betrayed spouse needs is not someone who is working hard to seem attuned. They need someone who is paying attention.

T - Turning Toward

Awareness without movement is incomplete. Turning toward is the behavioral expression of awareness — the moment when a partner registers a bid and responds in a way that says: I see you, and I am choosing to be here. In the Gottman research, the cumulative pattern of turning toward predicts relationship health more reliably than the presence or absence of conflict (Gottman & Silver, 2015). It is not a dramatic act. It is the ordinary, repeated choice to make contact rather than remain at a comfortable distance. For the unfaithful partner in active repair, this choice carries a weight that does not exist in ordinary relational life, because the betrayed spouse is not simply receiving a bid response. They are gathering evidence about whether this person, in this season, can be trusted to be there.

After betrayal, bids from the betrayed spouse often carry more emotional freight than they appear to. A question that sounds logistical may be a test of whether honesty is the new norm. A moment of vulnerability may be a probe for whether it is safe to be vulnerable. A withdrawal into silence may be a bid in its own right — an invitation to be sought out rather than left alone.

Gottman's research distinguishes three responses to bids: turning toward, which acknowledges the bid and offers some form of emotional presence; turning away, which ignores or misses the bid; and turning against, which responds with irritation, dismissal, or hostility (Gottman & Silver, 2015). The distinction matters more than it might seem. Turning against a bid, even once, carries disproportionate relational weight after betrayal. For a partner who is already operating from a position of disrupted safety, a dismissive response to a moment of vulnerability is not merely unpleasant. It reactivates the neural circuitry of threat. It confirms, at a level below conscious reasoning, that the person they are trying to trust is not safe to lean toward.

For the unfaithful partner, this means that responsiveness after betrayal requires a level of intentionality that is not characteristic of how most people function in ordinary relational life. The default patterns that allowed bids to slip by unnoticed, that responded to a partner's distress with a suggestion or a deflection, that treated emotional expression as a problem to be solved rather than an experience to be shared, need to be replaced with something more deliberate. This does not mean performing an exaggerated emotional display. It means developing the habit of pausing, registering, and responding to what is being communicated beneath the surface of an interaction.

T - Tolerance

Attunement does not require agreement, and it does not require resolution. Gottman's inclusion of tolerance in the ATTUNE framework reflects a finding that runs through decades of relational research: the couples with the most durable emotional connection are not the ones who share identical emotional responses to difficulty. They are the ones who can hold space for the other person's experience without needing to correct, redirect, or move it toward a conclusion (Gottman, 2011). After betrayal, tolerance becomes an act of discipline. The unfaithful partner who can remain present to a partner's grief without steering it toward its end — who can tolerate the discomfort of being the cause of suffering they cannot quickly repair, is practicing one of the more demanding forms of care available in this work.

U - Understanding

Understanding, in the Gottman framework, means more than comprehension of facts. It means entering the other person's experience with enough curiosity and care that they feel received rather than efficiently processed. Gottman (2011) describes this as responding with the heart before the head — before problem-solving, before reassuring, before explaining, acknowledging what is being felt. For the betrayed spouse, the experience of being understood — not managed, not redirected, but accompanied inside the experience — is one of the earliest perceptible signals that the repair is happening in more than words. It is also, Gottman notes, what the commitment of attuned partners sounds like made audible: "When you are in pain, the world stops and I listen" (Gottman & Silver, 2015, p. 103).

N – Nondefensive Listening

The capacity to receive expressions of pain, anger, or grief from a partner without responding defensively is, in the aftermath of betrayal, the component most likely to determine whether the other five hold. Nondefensive listening means being able to hear "You destroyed my ability to trust anyone, including myself" and not counterattacking, not withdrawing, not re-routing the conversation toward the unfaithful partner's own suffering, and not treating the expression of pain as an attack that must be neutralized.

This is extraordinarily difficult. The unfaithful partner is often carrying considerable shame, and shame is a notoriously unstable state. The movement from shame to defensiveness is rapid and largely automatic. When the shame becomes unbearable, the system looks for relief, and relief often arrives in the form of a counternarrative: *I've already apologized. This has been going on for months. Can't you see that I'm trying? When is enough going to be enough?*

Each of these defensive moves, however understandable, functions as a withdrawal from the very connection that repair requires. They signal to the betrayed spouse that their pain is too large for the other person to hold, that expressing it will result in their being managed rather than met. Over time, a betrayed spouse who receives consistent defensiveness in response to their grief will stop bringing it. That apparent peace is not healing. It is silence born of resignation.

The Gottman model addresses this through a framework for processing conflict that includes what Gottman calls accepting influence, allowing a partner's perspective to affect your own understanding and softened startup, which refers to the betrayed spouse's capacity to raise difficult feelings without leading with contempt or global accusations (Gottman & Silver, 2015). Both elements matter, but they are not symmetrical after betrayal. The unfaithful partner cannot expect a grieving partner to manage their expressions of pain according to the norms of emotionally healthy conflict when the relationship is still in active trauma. The primary work of nondefensive listening belongs, in the Atone and early Attune phases, to the unfaithful partner.

E - Empathy

The final component of the ATTUNE model is the one most people reach for first, and the one that means least when the others are absent. Empathy without awareness, turning toward, tolerance, and understanding becomes another form of performance: the emotion is expressed, but nothing has landed. What the Gottman research identifies as effective empathy is not the verbal expression of feeling but the communication of resonance the transmission, through word and sustained presence, that the other person's inner world has reached you and moved you (Gottman, 2011). Empathy, in this sense, is not manufactured. It is what remains when the defensive self has been set aside long enough to let another person's reality arrive.

The Asymmetry of Early Repair

The question of fairness arises with considerable force in the Attune phase. The emotional labor required in early repair is not equally distributed between partners. The unfaithful partner is being asked to do most of the active emotional work during this period: to remain present to pain they caused, to answer questions they would rather not be asked, to manage their own shame without redirecting it toward the betrayed spouse, to sustain the effort of attunement on an irregular schedule that does not correspond to when they feel emotionally ready. This is demanding work. It does not feel fair to many unfaithful partners, especially those who experienced their own pain and disconnection inside the marriage in the period leading up to the affair.

The betrayed spouse is also working. They are navigating grief, managing a dysregulated nervous system, attempting to make decisions about a future that cannot yet be clearly seen, and doing all of this while remaining in proximity to the person who caused the harm. This is not passive endurance. It is its own form of labor.

But the work is not the same work, and the demand placed on the unfaithful partner in early repair is correctly heavier. This asymmetry is not punitive. It reflects the structure of the injury. The betrayed spouse's nervous system and attachment system were disrupted by the affair, not by anything they chose to do. The unfaithful partner's willingness to absorb more discomfort during this period is not a concession. It is a form of accountability made concrete. It is one of the ways that the Atone phase becomes, over time, the Attune phase.

The unfaithful partner's willingness to absorb more discomfort during this period is not a concession. It is a form of accountability made concrete.

Esther Perel, psychotherapist and author of "The State of Affairs," whose work on infidelity has reached a wide audience, has noted something important about this asymmetry: the couple entering repair after an affair is, in a sense, two separate people with two separate desires. The betrayed spouse wants to repair the relationship they had, or something like it. The unfaithful partner is often, at some level, seeking something different, which may include the same relationship renewed but is sometimes a desire for a relationship that works differently than the one that existed before

(Perel, 2017). This divergence is not always conscious, and it is not always irreconcilable, but naming it matters because it affects how attunement work proceeds. If the unfaithful partner is working toward a different relational vision than the one the betrayed spouse is working to restore, the attunement gap will persist regardless of how skilled the effort becomes.

This is one of the reasons that couples doing this work with a skilled therapist are more likely to navigate it successfully. The asymmetry, the divergence in desire, and the demands of attunement are all easier to hold within a structured relational container than to manage entirely on one's own.

Conflict Without Retraumatization

One of the central challenges of the Attune phase is managing ongoing conflict in a relationship that is already carrying significant trauma. This is not a theoretical challenge. It is the practical reality of most couples who are attempting repair.

Even when the affair is fully disclosed and both partners are committed to rebuilding, the ordinary relational friction of shared life does not pause for the healing process. Decisions must be made, resentments arise, parenting disagreements emerge, financial pressures continue. And beneath all of it, the original injury is still present, still raw, capable of being activated by triggers that neither partner can fully anticipate.

The Gottman research has been particularly careful to distinguish between what Gottman calls solvable problems and perpetual problems in relationships (Gottman & Silver, 2015). Solvable problems are specific, often logistical, and have solutions.

Perpetual problems are rooted in the fundamental personality differences and value conflicts of two people, and they recur not because the couple is failing but because they are different. The research finding that most surprised the general public when it emerged is that approximately 69 percent of the conflicts couples bring to therapy are perpetual rather than solvable. They are not problems to be fixed. They are differences to be managed with mutual respect over time.

After betrayal, this already-challenging landscape becomes more complicated, because the unresolved injury functions as a perpetual presence in every conflict. A disagreement about how to handle a particular situation with a child can become, within moments, an activation of the original betrayal. Not because the couple is derailing purposely, but because the nervous system of the betrayed spouse has learned to treat relational threat as a signal that activates the original injury. The new conflict arrives carrying old weight.

Gottman's four destructive communication patterns, which he identified as predictors of relationship dissolution and labeled the Four Horsemen, are particularly relevant here: criticism (attacking character rather than behavior), contempt (expressing disgust or superiority), defensiveness (refusing to acknowledge responsibility), and stonewalling (emotionally withdrawing from the interaction) (Gottman & Levenson, 1992; Gottman & Silver, 2015). All four patterns are more likely to emerge under conditions of elevated physiological arousal, which means that couples navigating betrayal trauma are doing so in conditions that increase the probability of the very responses most damaging to their repair.

The Four Horsemen After Betrayal

Criticism: "You always put yourself first. That's why this happened."

Contempt: Dismissing a partner's expressed pain with eye-rolling, sarcasm, or mockery.

Defensiveness: "I've already apologized. Why do we keep having this conversation?"

Stonewalling: Shutting down emotionally when the conversation becomes too activating.

All four patterns are more damaging after betrayal than in ordinary conflict, because each one confirms the fear already present in the betrayed spouse: that their pain is too much, that they are not safe, that the person they are trying to trust will abandon or dismiss them when it matters most.

The antidotes to each of the Four Horsemen are well-documented in the Gottman research: replacing criticism with a gentle complaint that addresses specific behavior rather than character; replacing contempt with the cultivation of honest appreciation; replacing defensiveness with accountability; replacing stonewalling with a called time-out that includes a return to the conversation (Gottman & Silver, 2015). These antidotes are teachable. They are also harder to access when the arousal level in the nervous system is already elevated, which means that one of the most practical interventions available to couples in this phase is learning to recognize when they are too flooded to continue a productive conversation and to pause without that pause becoming a permanent withdrawal.

Gottman's research identifies a physiological threshold above which productive conversation is largely impossible: when heart rate exceeds approximately 100 beats per minute during conflict, the parts of the brain responsible for nuanced emotional processing are largely offline (Gottman, 2011). A person in this state cannot genuinely listen, cannot take in new information, and is likely to say things they will later regret or that will cause significant harm. Recognizing the onset of flooding and agreeing on a signal and a protocol for pausing when it occurs, is one of the most concrete and immediately useful skills couples doing repair work can develop.

This matters specifically for betrayal recovery because the betrayed spouse's flooding threshold is typically lower during active trauma, and the topics most likely to trigger flooding are the very topics that repair requires engaging. The work of the Attune phase includes developing a shared capacity to approach these topics gradually, with intentional nervous system regulation, rather than simply attempting to push through the flooding and hoping the conversation ends somewhere constructive.

The Trust Metric: Attunement as Evidence

There is a concept embedded in the Gottman research on trust that deserves more attention than it typically receives in popular treatments of the subject. Gottman distinguishes between what he calls metric trust and moral trust (Gottman, 2011). Moral trust is the abstract, global sense of whether a partner can be counted on to be faithful and honest. It is the kind of trust that is most directly ruptured by an affair. Metric trust is different. It is the operational, moment-to-moment sense of whether a partner is tracking my experience, caring about my needs, and responding to what matters to me in the specific transactions of everyday life.

The reason this distinction matters for the Attune phase is that metric trust, unlike moral trust, can begin to be rebuilt relatively early in the repair process, even before the deeper questions about the future of the relationship have been resolved. Every time the unfaithful partner turns toward a bid from the betrayed spouse, every time they remain present to expressed pain without deflecting it, every time they demonstrate that they have noticed something the betrayed spouse cares about and have responded to it with care, metric trust accumulates. Slowly, incrementally, in ways that do not resolve the large wound but do begin to create a different daily texture to the relationship.

Many betrayed spouses describe this accumulation before they have words for it. They say things like: "I don't know if I trust him yet, but I notice that he's different." Or: "She's actually listening now in a way she never did before, and I don't know what to do with that." These statements reflect the early accumulation of metric trust. They do not constitute full restoration of trust. But they represent something real, and their presence means that the underlying architecture for a different kind of relationship is beginning to form.

For the unfaithful partner, understanding the trust metric reframes the work of the Attune phase. The question is not simply "am I being honest enough" but "am I showing up consistently enough that my partner's nervous system is beginning to register safety." Honesty is necessary but not sufficient. What the betrayed spouse's nervous system and attachment system need is not primarily a performance review. They need enough repeated experiences of responsiveness that the default prediction begins to shift. This takes longer than most unfaithful partners expect and requires more consistency than most people can sustain without external support.

When Attunement Is New to the Relationship

Some couples working through the Attune phase face a specific challenge: the attunement being asked for is not something the relationship ever reliably had. The affair did not emerge in a context of emotional intimacy that was then broken. It emerged in a context where both partners were already, for various reasons, operating at significant emotional distance from each other.

This creates a particular kind of dissonance in the repair work. The betrayed spouse is being asked to receive attunement as evidence of repair from a partner who was never reliably attuned before the affair. The unfaithful partner is being asked to provide something they have no established habit of providing. And both partners are doing this work while the original injury is still present and the stakes are at their highest.

This does not make repair impossible. But it does mean that the Attune phase for these couples is not a restoration. It is a construction. They are not rebuilding something that was destroyed. They are building, in some respects, something that never fully existed. That is harder, and it is also, for some couples, the first genuinely honest reckoning with what their relationship was rather than what they needed it to be.

Esther Perel has written thoughtfully about the way an affair sometimes functions as an indicator of a desire for a different kind of relational life, not necessarily a different partner, but a more alive, present, and emotionally engaged way of being in the relationship one already has (Perel, 2017). This observation is not a defense of affairs, and it should not be used to assign responsibility for the affair to the betrayed spouse. Affairs are a choice made by the individual who made them, and the existence of relational problems does not create or justify that choice. But the observation is useful because it names something that can be addressed in the Attune phase: the construction of a relational culture that both partners want to live in. This is harder than restoring what existed before. It is also, for couples who are willing to do the deeper work, more meaningful.

The distinction between repair as restoration and repair as construction has practical implications for how couples approach therapy during this phase. A therapist who is working only to restore the pre-affair equilibrium may miss the ways in which that equilibrium was already part of the problem. A therapist who is attending to what each partner needs, wants, and is capable of in a sustainable relationship can help the couple navigate toward something different. Not every couple will find that the new construction is one both partners choose. But for those who do, it is a different foundation.

What Attunement Looks Like in Practice

The Gottman research offers a set of specific, observable attunement behaviors that distinguish couples who are rebuilding connection from couples who are maintaining the appearance of repair while remaining fundamentally disconnected. Several of these behaviors are particularly relevant to betrayal recovery.

Rituals of Connection

Gottman and his colleagues have identified the importance of what they call rituals of connection: recurring, intentional practices that create predictable moments of contact between partners (Gottman & Silver, 2015). These can be simple, such as a specific greeting at the beginning and end of each day, a brief check-in about the emotional state each partner is carrying, or a weekly conversation that is protected from logistical discussion and focused on how each person is doing. After betrayal, the purpose of these rituals is not primarily enjoyment. It is the construction of a reliable, recurring experience of the other person being present and interested. Over time, reliability is one of the building blocks of restored safety.

Expressed Appreciation and Admiration

One of the consistent predictors of relationship satisfaction in the Gottman research is the ratio of positive to negative interactions, a concept Gottman has sometimes described as the 5:1 ratio: for every negative interaction in a relationship, approximately five positive interactions are needed to maintain emotional equilibrium (Gottman & Silver, 2015). After betrayal, this ratio is typically severely disrupted. The overwhelming weight of negative affect, understandably, dominates.

The recovery of a positive interaction ratio after betrayal does not require pretending that things are fine. It requires the deliberate cultivation of appreciation, noticing what is admirable, useful, kind, or interesting about a partner, and saying it out loud.

For the betrayed spouse, this may feel counterintuitive or even dishonest when so much anger and grief are present. For the unfaithful partner, it may feel unearned, a form of asking for positive recognition in the middle of a repair process that they created the need for. Both resistances are understandable. The point is not to force positivity but to begin creating some of the relational texture that pure grief management cannot provide.

The Practice of Dreams Within Conflict

Among the more surprising findings from the Gottman research is the importance of what Gottman calls "dreams within conflict": the discovery, in the midst of ongoing disagreement, of the deeper hopes, fears, and values that animate each partner's position (Gottman & Silver, 2015). Couples who develop the capacity to ask each other "what matters to you about this, at the deepest level" tend to navigate perpetual problems with considerably more flexibility and respect than couples who remain focused exclusively on the surface position.

After betrayal, this skill has special relevance. Many of the recurring conflicts of the Attune phase are not really about the specific issue presenting. They are about the underlying fears that have been activated by the betrayal: fear of being abandoned, fear of being deceived again, fear of being inadequate, fear that the relationship is fundamentally unsafe. When a betrayed spouse escalates a conflict about a missed phone call into a larger confrontation about trustworthiness, this is not irrational. It reflects the fact that the missed phone call has activated a deeper fear. A partner who can recognize the fear beneath the conflict and respond to it directly rather than defending against the surface argument, is practicing one of the most sophisticated forms of attunement available.

* * *

Claire

Three months after Daniel completed what Claire had come to think of as the honesty work, something unexpected happened. Not a resolution, and not the reconciliation she was not yet ready for. Something smaller.

They had been sitting at the table after dinner, the children in bed, the house quiet. Claire was not sure she wanted to talk. Daniel had been consistent for long enough that she had stopped bracing against every evening. She was not at ease, exactly, but she was no longer operating entirely on the assumption that something was about to break.

She mentioned, without a particular agenda, that she had been thinking about her mother. That her mother was aging in ways that were starting to require attention. That she had been carrying the worry of it for a few weeks without quite knowing what to do with it.

Daniel did not offer a solution. He did not pivot to logistics. He turned toward her, put down what he was holding, and asked: "How long have you been carrying that?"

It was a small thing. In a healthy marriage, it would have been ordinary. In this marriage, in this season, it was not ordinary. It was the first time in months that Claire had extended something toward him that was not related to the affair or its aftermath, and he had caught it.

She told him about her mother. He listened for a long time. He asked, at one point, what she was most afraid of, and she answered honestly. He did not tell her not to worry.

When she went to bed that night, she lay in the dark for a long time. Not resolved. Not ready. But something had shifted. The person she had been trying to decide whether to trust was, in that hour, someone she recognized.

She did not tell him that. She did not know yet whether she trusted it to last.

But it had happened. That was something.

Evan

He began, in the sixth month, to watch her bids. His therapist had introduced him to the concept, the small, daily reaching-toward that signals: I want to be connected to you. She had asked him to pay attention, as an exercise, not to evaluate whether to respond but simply to observe: when does Amber reach toward you, and what happens when she does?

He watched for three weeks. He kept notes, because he was a person who kept notes.

What he found was a pattern he had not expected. Amber bid toward him, a question, a comment, a light touch on his arm as she passed consistently in the evenings before he had raised anything about the affair. When he initiated a conversation about what had happened, or about the ongoing questions he still needed answered, the bids stopped. Not immediately, not as a visible withdrawal. But in the hour after such a conversation, her availability dropped. She answered when spoken to. She did not reach.

He brought his notes to therapy. His therapist looked at them for a moment, then said: What do you see?

He said: She attunes toward the marriage she wants to have. She doesn't attune toward the one she has.

He sat with that for a while. It was not a final conclusion. People under pressure did not always have the capacity to remain present to pain that was, in part, their own doing. He understood this. He had read enough about shame and self-protection to know that the withdrawal was not necessarily a choice. But understanding the mechanism did not resolve the problem. He needed a partner who could stay in the room when the room was hard. So far, he could not be certain that was what he had.

* * *

The Danger of Attunement Theater

There is a pattern that sometimes emerges in the Attune phase because it can look like progress while preventing it. The pattern is what might be called attunement theater: the unfaithful partner learns the vocabulary and behavioral markers of emotional attunement, practices the specific responses that are associated with responsiveness, and presents these behaviors consistently enough that the betrayed spouse begins to feel something is shifting, only to discover, eventually, that the performance was precisely that. The behaviors were not rooted in genuine interest or care. They were a more sophisticated form of image management.

Attunement theater is difficult to detect because it borrows the surface features of responsiveness. The questions sound caring. Attentiveness looks real. The non-defensive responses to expressed pain appear authentic. And yet something does not land. The betrayed spouse may not be able to articulate immediately why the interaction feels hollow, but the felt sense of not being genuinely met is present. Over time, the gap between performed attunement and felt connection becomes harder to ignore.

The distinction between attunement and its performed counterpart is not always easy to see from the outside, and it is not always conscious in the unfaithful partner. Some partners who begin with performed responsiveness are learning, and the performance gradually becomes a habit that then becomes something more rooted. But for others, the performance is in the service of a specific goal, such as ending the repair process sooner, re-establishing normalcy, or managing the betrayed spouse's distress to reduce discomfort rather than addressing it.

One of the ways a skilled therapist provides value in this phase is in attending to exactly this distinction, supporting the unfaithful partner's development of internal attunement rather than just the behaviors that resemble it, and helping the betrayed spouse distinguish between shifts that are real and responses that are still primarily self-protective.

For readers who are doing this work without therapeutic support, the clearest signal available is the consistency of responsiveness across contexts and moods. A partner who is developing attunement will show it in the small moments as well as the large ones, when nothing is at stake as well as when they know they are being evaluated, when it is inconvenient as well as when it is easy.

A Word to the Reader Who Is Not Receiving This

Some readers of this chapter will recognize in the attunement research a description of something they have never experienced in their relationship and are not experiencing now. Some will have a partner who is actively resisting the repair process, who meets expressions of pain with annoyance or withdrawal, who shows up for the behaviors most likely to be visible to the outside world while remaining essentially unchanged in the private interior of the relationship.

This is not a failure on your part. The capacity to attune, in the real and sustained sense the Gottman research describes, is a skill and a practice, and not everyone comes to it willingly or quickly. It can be developed in therapy, with the right kind of support, over a longer timeline than most betrayed spouses would choose. It cannot be compelled. It cannot be achieved by the betrayed partner working harder or needing less or becoming easier to be with.

What you can do is be clear with yourself about what you are actually receiving, as distinct from what you are hoping for or have been promised. The attunement work described in this chapter is not an aspirational standard designed to make real relationships feel inadequate. It is a description of what emotional repair looks like, grounded in research on what changes the trajectory of relationships over time. If what you are receiving does not resemble it, that is worth knowing. It affects the decisions you may need to make about how you will take care of yourself and what conditions, if any, you are willing to continue offering to this repair process.

Your healing does not depend on your partner becoming someone who is capable of this work. The grief of that, if it is your situation, is its own legitimate grief. It deserves to be honored rather than explained away.

A Reflection: On Being Known

> You have searched me and known me. You know when I sit and when I rise; you perceive my thoughts from afar. You discern my going out and my lying down; you are familiar with all my ways.
>
> Psalm 139:1-3 (NIV)

There is a human longing that runs beneath the attunement research and emerges most clearly in moments like the one described in Psalm 139: the longing to be fully known. Not managed. Not observed from a careful distance. Known, in the way that the psalmist describes God knowing him, with a familiarity that reaches beneath performance, beneath the self-presentation offered to the world, beneath even the thoughts one can articulate to oneself.

This longing is one of the reasons betrayal is so devastating. The intimacy of a marriage, at its best, is the place where this kind of knowing was meant to be possible. The affair does not simply betray the loyalty of a partner. It reveals that the knowing was, for a period of time, incomplete. That a significant part of the self the unfaithful partner carried through the world was hidden from the person who was supposed to see them most clearly. That the intimacy that felt most honest may have been, in some respects, carefully curated.

For people of faith, the Psalm offers something worth sitting with. It is possible to be fully known by the one who searches and perceives and is familiar with all our ways, and to survive that knowing, even to rest in it. The God of this Psalm is not undone by the complexity of what is discovered. The knowledge is not the prelude to rejection. It is the ground of relationship.

This matters for the repair work in specific ways. The betrayed spouse who is trying to decide whether to trust again carries, underneath the relational question, a deeper question: Is it safe to be known? The answer given by the affair is: not entirely, not fully, not in the place I most expected it to be possible. The work of the Attune phase, at its deepest, is the slow re-establishment of conditions in which that question can be answered differently, in which being known in the relationship is met not with the threat of harm but with care.

That work is not completed by theology. But for the person whose faith has been a source of grounding through the rest of the repair process, the Psalm offers a different kind of company for the waiting. You are known by the one whose knowledge does not wound. That does not replace what was lost. But it holds something real.

Looking Ahead

The Attune phase of repair does not have a clean ending. It does not conclude when a certain number of attunement skills have been practiced or a certain amount of time has passed. It becomes, gradually, the culture of the relationship: the ongoing, imperfect, effortful practice of turning toward each other rather than away.

The next chapter of this book moves into the third phase of the Gottman repair model: Attach. Where Atone was about accountability and Attune is about connection, Attach is about the reconstruction of a shared life that is not simply haunted by what happened but is organized around different values, different practices, and a different kind of honesty than the relationship had before. The Attach phase is the longest work, and in some ways the least dramatic. It is the work of Tuesday afternoons and ordinary disagreements and the gradual, real discovery that the relationship you are living in is not just the repaired version of the one that was damaged but something that has been renegotiated, with more honesty, from a more realistic foundation.

For couples who reach this phase with work behind them, the view is different than the one they had at the beginning. Not because the pain has been erased. Because it has been held, honestly, by two people who have chosen to keep facing it together.

References

Gottman, J. M. (2011). *The science of trust: Emotional attunement for couples*. W. W. Norton.

Gottman, J. M., & Levenson, R. W. (1992). Marital processes predictive of later dissolution: Behavior, physiology, and health. *Journal of Personality and Social Psychology*, 63(2), 221–233. https://doi.org/10.1037/0022-3514.63.2.221

Gottman, J. M., & Silver, N. (2015). *The seven principles for making marriage work: A practical guide from the country's foremost relationship expert* (Rev. ed.). Harmony Books.

Perel, E. (2017). *The state of affairs: Rethinking infidelity*. Harper.

Chapter Nine: Attach: Building A Relationship Worth Keeping

"We must be willing to get rid of the life we've planned, so as to have the life that is waiting for us."

— Joseph Campbell, Reflections on the Art of Living (1991)

Claire

Somewhere around month eighteen, Claire noticed something she could not immediately explain. She and Daniel had been in couples therapy for more than a year. He had answered her questions, most of them, and had stopped defending himself against the ones she repeated. He had told the truth, as far as she could determine, about how the affair had started and how long it had continued. He had begun, tentatively and with more stumbling than she would have preferred, to respond to her pain as something that needed his attention rather than his management.

And yet something felt incomplete. Not broken, exactly. Not the raw-wound quality of the first months, when getting through a single day required effort she could barely sustain. This was different. A kind of suspended quality. Like a piece of music that has resolved most of its dissonance but has not yet found its final chord.

She brought this to her therapist, who asked her: "What would it mean if this relationship were good again? Not repaired. Not functional. Good?"

Claire sat with that question for a long time. She realized, slowly, that she had spent eighteen months learning to survive the damage. She had stabilized, grieved, demanded accountability, watched carefully for patterns, and rebuilt something that felt, most days, like solid ground beneath her feet. What she had not done, and perhaps had not believed was possible, was decide what she wanted the relationship to become.

That was the beginning of the Attach phase. Not a new start, exactly, because you cannot erase what happened. But the beginning of a different question: not only Can this be repaired? but What kind of relationship do we want to build, and is building it together worth what it will require?

Evan

Around month eighteen, Evan's couples therapist asked them a question. She asked them each to answer it separately, on paper, without consulting the other. The question was: What do you want this relationship to become?

He wrote for several minutes. He wanted honesty, as a real baseline rather than a standard invoked when convenient. He wanted a shared account of what had happened, not a version calibrated for his feelings, but the actual account. He wanted to stop living inside the sensation of holding a map that had known errors he could not yet locate. He wanted to trust the person he was sleeping next to. He wanted the story to have stopped changing.

He was given Amber's answer to read. She wanted to move forward. She wanted to rebuild. She wanted to stop living in the crisis of the past eighteen months and invest in the future they had planned. She wrote three paragraphs about the things she valued in their marriage. His stability. His patience. His commitment.

He noticed what she had not written. She had not written "I want to give you the full truth." She had not written "I want to become someone you can trust." She had not written anything that required her to produce something she had not yet produced.

He handed the paper back to the therapist without saying anything. She looked at him and asked: What are you noticing?

He said: She wrote about what she wants from the marriage. I wrote about what I need for the marriage to exist.

There was a long silence. He did not fill it. He had learned, over the past year, that some silences carried more information than whatever he might say into them.

* * *

The Gottman Institute's model of affair recovery describes three phases: Atone, Attune, and Attach. The first two phases have been addressed in the preceding chapters. Atone is the work of real accountability, the cessation of deception, the full reckoning with harm done, and the behavioral commitments that make trust repair possible. Attune is the work of rebuilding emotional connection, the capacity to turn toward rather than away, to register what a partner is feeling and respond in ways that make them feel met rather than processed.

Attach is the third phase, and it is in some ways the hardest to describe because it is the least dramatic. It does not have the urgent quality of the Atone phase, with its disclosures and accountability conversations and the pressing question of whether the affair is truly over. It does not have the tenderness of early attunement work, the first moments when a couple discovers that they can still reach each other. The Attach phase is quieter. It is the long middle distance of repair, the work of constructing, together, a relationship that is not simply the old one patched over but something deliberately renegotiated.

For many couples, this is where they run out of map. The crisis has passed. The immediate wound has been addressed. The therapeutic work has produced real change. And yet, neither partner is quite sure what they are building, or how to build it, or whether what they are building will be worth the years it will take to complete.

This chapter is about that work. It addresses how couples move from the crisis of betrayal toward a renewed relationship, what that rebuilding requires, how trust gradually shifts from fragile to durable, what research tells us about the conditions under which couples who survive affairs go on to build something strong, and what honest hope looks like at this stage of the journey.

From Surviving to Building

There is a threshold that many couples in affair recovery cross without recognizing it: the shift from crisis management to real construction. The crisis phase is defined by its urgency. Every day brings new information to process, new pain to contain, new assessments of risk and safety and intent. The work of the crisis phase is essentially defensive: How do I protect myself? How do I assess what is actually happening? How do I keep functioning while my world has been restructured without my consent?

The construction phase asks different questions. It assumes a degree of stability that was not present in the acute months. It assumes that basic safety has been established, that the affair has ended, that the unfaithful partner has demonstrated at least a working commitment to honesty and accountability, and that the betrayed spouse has developed enough internal regulation to bring sustained intention to the work of repair rather than simply surviving each day as it comes. These are real assumptions, and they are not met equally by all couples, or on the same timeline.

But when they are met, even partially, the orientation of the work changes. The question becomes less What do I need to survive this? and more What do we want to become?

The Attach phase does not ask you to forget what happened. It asks something harder: to decide, with clear eyes, what kind of relationship is worth the years it will take to rebuild.

John Gottman's research on what distinguishes couples who fully recover from affairs from those who remain stuck in a cycle of recurring crisis identified several consistent factors. The couples who achieved what he called "the recovery" were not those who had somehow avoided the pain of betrayal. They had faced it fully. What distinguished them was, in part, the degree to which they eventually developed a shared narrative about what had happened, a mutual understanding of the vulnerabilities and failures that had allowed the affair to occur, and a joint commitment to constructing a relationship organized around different values than the one that had been damaged (Gottman & Gottman, 2017; Gottman & Silver, 2012).

That shared narrative does not minimize harm. It does not distribute blame equally or suggest that the affair was anyone's fault but the person who chose it. What it does is give the couple a way of understanding their own history, which is honest enough to support real change. Without it, repair tends to be surface level: the behaviors improve, the acute crisis fades, but neither partner has a clear account of what went wrong or a deliberate intention about what they are building together.

What the Attach Phase Actually Requires

The Attach phase is not a single task. It is a cluster of overlapping processes that happen simultaneously over an extended period of time. The following are the ones that research and clinical observation identify as most central to lasting renewal rather than surface-level stability.

A Shared and Honest Account of What Happened

One of the features of betrayal trauma that persists longest is the fragmented quality of the betrayed spouse's understanding of what occurred. Full disclosure is rarely delivered in a single conversation. Most betrayed spouses spend months, sometimes years, assembling a picture from partial information, evasive answers, and the slow emergence of details that were initially minimized or withheld. The result is a narrative that has gaps, and those gaps remain live wounds long after the relationship has otherwise stabilized.

The Attach phase, when it is proceeding well, includes a consolidation of the account. This does not mean revisiting every painful detail indefinitely. It means that both partners have arrived at a shared understanding that is honest enough to rest on. The unfaithful partner has told the truth, fully enough that the betrayed spouse is not haunted by the certainty that there is more they do not know. The story of what happened, why it happened, and what it revealed about the relationship has been faced together.

Research by Gordon, Baucom, and Snyder (2004) on the treatment of extramarital affairs identified narrative coherence as one of the key markers distinguishing couples who achieved real recovery from those who remained in chronic relational distress. Couples who could articulate, with some shared understanding, what had led to the affair and what had changed in response to it were significantly more likely to report sustained improvement in relationship satisfaction than those who had achieved behavioral stability without the narrative work.

For some couples, this narrative work happens naturally through sustained therapy. For others, it requires a more deliberate conversation: a moment when both partners sit together, not to relitigate what happened but to say, as honestly as they can, This is what I understand about how we got here, and this is what I understand about what it will take not to return. That conversation is uncomfortable. It also tends to be one of the most important ones a couple in this phase can have.

Renegotiating the Terms of the Relationship

One of the more counterintuitive findings in the affair recovery literature is that some couples who go through the work of repair describe their post-affair relationship as, in meaningful ways, better than what preceded the crisis. Not immediately, and not without grief for what it cost. But better in the sense of being more honest, more deliberate, more deliberately organized around what each partner needs rather than around the assumptions that had accumulated over years without being examined.

This is not a silver-lining argument. The affair did not need to happen for the relationship to improve. Many couples achieve the same honest renegotiation without betrayal. The point is not that crisis is necessary for growth but that the Attach phase offers, for couples who are fully doing the work, an unusual opportunity to ask questions that are rarely asked in otherwise stable marriages: What do we want from this relationship? What were the parts of our life together that were working, and what were the parts that were quietly not? What do we each need that we were not asking for or receiving?

These are difficult questions in any context. They are harder still in the aftermath of betrayal, where the temptation to attribute all problems to the affair, or to avoid the entire subject of the relationship's history to reduce conflict, is strong. But the couples who move through the Attach phase most fully are typically the ones who do not skip this work, who bring the same willingness to look clearly at their relational patterns that they brought to examining the affair itself.

Shirley Glass's research observed that couples who achieved recovery often described changes not only in the unfaithful partner's behavior but in the relationship's fundamental culture: how conflicts were handled, how needs were communicated, how much of the real interior life of each partner was visible to the other (Glass, 2003). The walls-and-windows model she developed to describe how affairs grow, the reversal of transparency inward and protection outward, implies a corrective: real repair involves not just the cessation of the reversed configuration but the construction of a new one, in which openness is deliberately organized toward the primary relationship.

Trust: How It Actually Rebuilds

One of the most common misconceptions about trust repair is that it is primarily about the passage of time. It is not. Time is a necessary but insufficient condition. What rebuilds trust is the accumulation of trustworthy behavior, consistently demonstrated over an extended period, in the full range of contexts the relationship includes: not only the high-visibility moments of reconciliation and apology but the ordinary, unobserved moments when a partner could choose deception or selfishness and does not.

Gottman's concept of the "trust metric" is useful here. In his research, trust is not primarily a cognitive assessment, a decision to believe what a partner says. It is an accumulated pattern of relational prediction: the degree to which a partner's behavior across many interactions has demonstrated that their interests are oriented toward the relationship rather than against it (Gottman, 2011). Betrayal destroys this metric comprehensively. Repair requires rebuilding it from a starting point of zero, not by declaration but by the slow accumulation of evidence.

For the betrayed spouse, this means that the rebuilding of trust is an ongoing assessment process that cannot be rushed. Hypervigilance in the early months of repair is not pathology. It is the nervous system appropriately tracking the evidence that the trust metric requires. As the evidence accumulates, as the unfaithful partner's behavior proves consistent across moods and circumstances and pressure, as the betrayed spouse's own internal regulation becomes more stable, the vigilance naturally reduces. Not because it was suppressed but because it no longer needs to be active at the same intensity.

Trust is not rebuilt in grand gestures. It is rebuilt in ordinary moments, accumulated over time, in which one person's behavior answers the question: Am I safe here?

This process has a meaningful neurobiological dimension. Research on trauma recovery has documented that the threat-response system, once sensitized by serious betrayal, does not simply return to its pre-trauma baseline when the threat is resolved. It requires its own repair process, which is distinct from the relational repair process even though they interact with each other (van der Kolk, 2014). For some betrayed spouses, working with a skilled trauma therapist alongside couples therapy produces significantly better outcomes than either treatment alone, because the internal repair and the relational repair are different, and both require attention.

Intimacy After Betrayal

Few aspects of the Attach phase are more fraught for couples than the question of physical and emotional intimacy. For many betrayed spouses, sexual intimacy in the aftermath of an affair is complicated by associations that did not exist before: images, comparisons, questions about what the unfaithful partner may have done or said or felt in the affair. The body carries the betrayal in ways that are not simply resolved by a decision to move forward. What felt natural and safe before has become uncertain territory.

There is no universal timeline for this, and any framework that imposes one should be treated with suspicion. Some couples find that physical reconnection is an important part of their healing, and that the return of honest, unhurried intimacy is one of the most meaningful markers of recovery. Others find that they need to move much more slowly, that the capacity for physical vulnerability rebuilds well behind the capacity for emotional vulnerability, and that rushing the process for the sake of normalcy produces the opposite of what is intended.

What the research on post-affair intimacy consistently emphasizes is the importance of genuine consent and of the absence of coercion, direct or subtle (Baucom et al., 2009). The betrayed spouse's readiness for physical intimacy is not a metric for whether the relationship is progressing. An unfaithful partner who treats their betrayed spouse's reluctance as an obstacle to be overcome, rather than as a reasonable response that deserves patient honoring, has not yet understood what real repair requires.

Emotional intimacy in the Attach phase looks different than it did before the affair, and for most couples, which is not a loss. Before the affair, intimacy was often assumed rather than chosen: the comfortable proximity of people who have been together long enough that they no longer think very carefully about what they are giving each other. In the Attach phase, intimacy becomes more deliberate. The choice to be emotionally present to a partner, to be honest about what you are carrying, to ask what your partner needs and mean it, these are choices that have been stripped of their automatic quality. What remains requires intention. For many couples, that intentionality is one of the lasting gifts of the repair work, even if accepting it as a gift feels complicated given what it cost.

The Lasting Effects of Betrayal, and Honest Hope

No account of affair recovery is complete without honesty about its limits. The research literature on couples who survive infidelity and achieve real repair is, on balance, more encouraging than many people expect. Studies consistently find that a meaningful proportion of couples who do the sustained work of recovery report high levels of relationship satisfaction at long-term follow-up, sometimes higher than comparable couples who have not experienced infidelity (Snyder et al., 2007). The assumption that an affair permanently and irreparably damages a marriage is not supported by the evidence.

But the same research is clear that recovery, even when real, does not produce a return to the pre-affair baseline. It produces something different. For most couples who successfully repair, the relationship that emerges is changed in ways that are both costly and, paradoxically, sometimes valuable. The costs are real: a loss of innocence about what was possible between them, a permanent awareness of vulnerability that was not present before, the knowledge that they have been tested in a way they cannot unknow. These costs do not disappear with time. They become part of the texture of the relationship.

The gains, when they occur, are also real. A greater honesty about needs and limits. A more deliberate quality to the choice to be together. A capacity for emotional conversation that may never have existed before the crisis forced it into existence. Couples who describe their repaired relationship as truly good almost never describe it as the same as what preceded the betrayal. They describe it as harder-won, more honest, and in some important ways more real.

There is also a set of effects that research has documented in betrayed spouses that do not simply resolve even in the context of successful repair. Jennifer Freyd's work on betrayal trauma theory notes that betrayal by a close attachment figure produces a distinct wound, distinct from other forms of trauma, because it occurs at the intersection of threat and dependency (Freyd, 1994; Freyd & Birrell, 2013). The person who harmed you is also, at least at the time of discovery, the person you depend on most deeply. That combination leaves traces that are not simply erased by subsequent good behavior.

What this practically means is that some betrayed spouses who have done real repair work, who are in relationships that by every observable measure have been measurably restored, still carry a sensitivity that their pre-affair selves did not have. A sharpened alertness to inconsistency. A faster activation when something feels uncertain or withholding. A grief that surfaces at unexpected moments, months or years after the acute crisis has passed.

This is not a sign that repair has failed. It is the honest signature of serious harm. The nervous system that was shaped by the experience of betrayal does not become exactly what it was before, any more than a bone that has healed from a fracture is indistinguishable from one that has never broken. The healed version is real, and functional, and often strong. It is also different. That difference deserves to be honored rather than treated as evidence of insufficient recovery.

When the Work Is Not Mutual

The Attach phase, as described in the Gottman model, is inherently a joint endeavor. Both partners are building together: toward a shared narrative, toward deliberate intimacy, toward a relationship organized around honesty and real accountability. This vision assumes that both people are fully in the work, motivated by more than fear or obligation, and willing to do the internal labor that honest renegotiation requires.

For many people reading this chapter, that assumption does not hold. Some readers are in relationships where the unfaithful partner has offered enough to reduce the acute crisis but not enough to constitute real repair. Where accountability was partial and is now considered closed. Where the therapy has been discontinued because things seem fine, meaning the immediate conflict has reduced but the underlying work has not been done. Where the betrayed spouse continues to grieve and question while the unfaithful partner has, in their own assessment, moved on.

The Attach phase cannot be completed alone. It can be approached alone, in the sense that a betrayed spouse can do sustained personal work toward their own healing and integration regardless of what their partner chooses. But the relational renegotiation, the construction of a new shared understanding, the deliberate rebuilding of intimacy and trust, these require two people who are both present to the work. One person doing the work while the other is absent, resistant, or present only in performance produces a distinct exhaustion worth naming.

If this is your situation, the most important thing you can do is be honest with yourself about what you are building, as distinct from what you are hoping the other person is building alongside you. Some partners arrive at real repair slowly, and with much more prompting and resistance than would be ideal. The question is not whether the pace is inconvenient but whether the direction is real. A partner who is moving, however imperfectly, toward the relational honesty the Attach phase requires is different from one who has simply stopped being in active crisis mode while the deeper repair remains undone.

The clarity that distinguishes these two cases is worth pursuing, even when it is uncomfortable. A skilled therapist can help you see the difference from a less emotionally entangled position than you are likely to be able to achieve alone. If continued individual or couples therapy is not currently available to you, the chapters on safety and decision-making earlier in this book offer frameworks for assessing what you are receiving versus what real repair looks like.

The Long Work

One of the most important things to know about the Attach phase is that it does not have a clear ending. Unlike the Atone phase, which reaches a kind of conclusion when full disclosure has been given and the specific behaviors of accountability have been established, or the Attune phase, which has a more identifiable turning point when real emotional connection has been reestablished, the Attach phase is the ongoing work of a relationship.

In this sense, it is not unlike the work of any marriage that is taking itself seriously: the regular tending of the connection, the willingness to revisit assumptions and renegotiate terms as circumstances change, the ongoing practice of turning toward rather than away. What distinguishes the post-affair version is the higher baseline of intentionality it requires, at least for several years, and the heightened sensitivity both partners bring to any sign that the old patterns might be reasserting themselves.

Many couples who have done real repair work describe a moment, usually somewhere between two and five years after discovery, when the relationship stops feeling primarily organized around the recovery from the affair and begins to feel primarily organized around the present. The affair becomes part of the couple's history rather than the dominant frame of their present. This does not mean forgetting, and it does not mean that the sensitivity disappears entirely. It means that the weight of the present relationship has become substantial enough that the past, though not erased, no longer has the same gravitational pull.

That shift does not happen automatically. It is the accumulated result of years of the practices the Gottman research identifies as central to relational health: consistent turning toward bids for connection, effective conflict management that does not allow gridlock to calcify into contempt, the regular investment in the relationship's shared meaning and friendship (Gottman & Silver, 1999). What is true for any healthy marriage is equally true for the repaired one. The difference is that the couple who has been through betrayal tends to do this work with more deliberate awareness of what is at stake than the couple who has not been tested in the same way.

A Different Path

Not every couple who arrives at this phase of recovery stays together, and it is important to hold that honestly. The work described in this chapter, if both partners engage it fully, often produces a relationship worth keeping. But the same clarity that real repair work requires can also produce, in some cases, a different kind of honesty: the recognition that what was damaged cannot be rebuilt, or that the relationship that would emerge from rebuilding is not one either partner actually wants.

For some betrayed spouses, the Attach phase arrives as the moment when it becomes clear, with grief and without self-deception, that they do not want to build a life with this person. Not because the betrayal cannot be forgiven, but because the honest accounting of what the relationship was, what it required to sustain, and what it would require going forward does not produce, after full reckoning, a desire to continue. This is a legitimate place to arrive. It is not failure. It is, in its way, a different kind of integrity.

The decision to leave a marriage after sustained repair work has been attempted is not the same as the decision made in the acute crisis phase, when neither partner had full information or the emotional stability to assess clearly. It is a more considered decision, made with the benefit of what has been learned and with grief for what was good before it was damaged. It deserves to be honored as such, not treated as evidence that the recovery work was wasted. The work was not wasted. It produced the clarity on which the decision rests.

A Reflection: On Beginning Again

> Behold, I am doing a new thing; now it springs forth, do you not perceive it? I will make a way in the wilderness and rivers in the desert.
>
> Isaiah 43:19 (ESV)

There is a different kind of faith required not in crisis, when the intensity of the moment produces its own kind of certainty, but in the long middle distance of a work that is proceeding but not yet finished. The faith that what is being built is worth the building. The faith that the pain has not been meaningless. The faith that the changes that have occurred are real enough to rest on, even when the evidence is still accumulating.

The verse from Isaiah speaks into that kind of moment. It is addressed to people in exile, to those who have been removed from the life they knew and are not yet in sight of what comes next. The assurance it offers is not that the wilderness is comfortable, or that the road through it is well-marked, or that the duration will be short. It is that something new is already in motion, and that it is possible, if you pay close attention, to perceive it.

For people of faith who are somewhere in the middle of the Attach phase, the Isaiah text offers something more precise than general encouragement. The phrase "a way in the wilderness" does not promise an absence of wilderness. It promises a way through it. The new thing being done is not the erasure of what was damaged but the opening of a path that did not exist before.

This is not a passage that should be used to rush the process or to suggest that spiritual optimism is a substitute for the slow, concrete work of rebuilding. Willard's (2002) observation that spiritual formation is always concrete and embodied, never merely interior or aspirational, applies with special force here. The new thing that is springing forth in a recovering relationship is not invisible or purely spiritual. It shows up in behavior, in honesty, in the quality of presence two people bring to each other on an ordinary Wednesday.

But for those who find in their faith a resource for the long work, the Isaiah text offers something the clinical literature alone cannot: the assurance that being in a process of real renewal is not a sign of inadequacy. It is, in its way, the shape that faithfulness sometimes takes. The work is not finished. The destination is not yet fully visible. And moving forward in that condition, with honesty and care and the willingness to be surprised by what is being built, is its own kind of faithfulness.

Looking Ahead

The three phases of the Gottman repair model, Atone, Attune, and Attach, have been the organizing framework for Part Three of this book. They describe a sequence that is real but not rigid: couples move through these phases unevenly, sometimes returning to earlier work while simultaneously doing later work, sometimes finding that a phase they thought was complete requires revisiting when new information surfaces or old wounds are reopened by circumstances.

What the framework offers is not a guaranteed progression but a map of what real repair involves. Each phase addresses a different dimension of what was damaged by the affair: Atone addresses the breach of integrity, Attune addresses the breach of emotional connection, and Attach addresses the question that remains when both of those have been faced: What kind of relationship are you building, and are you building it deliberately enough to sustain it?

The remaining chapters of this book turn to questions that exist alongside the repair framework rather than within it: the challenges facing betrayed spouses who are healing without a willing partner, the long-term effects of betrayal that persist even in successful recoveries, the question of forgiveness and what it actually means and requires, and the final chapter on what it means to live forward, whether you have stayed in your marriage, left it, or are still holding the question in the honest uncertainty where it sometimes belongs.

The work described in this chapter is long. It is not finished in the reading of it. But it is also real, and it is possible, and the couples who have done it, with patience and honesty and willingness to be changed by what they faced, are the evidence that the map points somewhere worth going.

References

Campbell, J. (1991). *Reflections on the art of living: A Joseph Campbell companion* (D. K. Osbon, Ed.). HarperCollins.

Freyd, J. J. (1994). Betrayal trauma: Traumatic amnesia as an adaptive response to childhood abuse. *Ethics & Behavior, 4*(4), 307–329.

Freyd, J. J., & Birrell, P. (2013). *Blind to betrayal: Why we fool ourselves we aren't being fooled.* Wiley.

Glass, S. P. (2003). *Not "just friends": Rebuilding trust and recovering your sanity after infidelity.* Free Press.

Gordon, K. C., Baucom, D. H., & Snyder, D. K. (2004). An integrative intervention for promoting recovery from extramarital affairs. *Journal of Marital and Family Therapy, 30*(2), 213–231. https://doi.org/10.1111/j.1752-0606.2004.tb01235.x

Gottman, J. M. (2011). *The science of trust: Emotional attunement for couples.* W. W. Norton.

Gottman, J. M., & Gottman, J. S. (2017). *Treating affairs and trauma: A Gottman approach for therapists on the treatment of affairs and posttraumatic stress.* Gottman Institute.

Gottman, J. M., & Silver, N. (1999). *The seven principles for making marriage work.* Crown Publishers.

Gottman, J. M., & Silver, N. (2012). *What makes love last? How to build trust and avoid betrayal.* Simon & Schuster.

Snyder, D. K., Baucom, D. H., & Gordon, K. C. (2007). *Getting past the affair: A program to help you cope, heal, and move on—together or apart.* Guilford Press.

van der Kolk, B. A. (2014). *The body keeps the score: Brain, mind, and body in the healing of trauma.* Viking.

Willard, D. (2002). *Renovation of the heart: Putting on the character of Christ.* NavPress.

Part 4: The Long Work

Chapter Ten: What Lingers: The Long Tail of Betrayal

"The wound is the place where the Light enters you."
— attributed to Rumi

Claire

Three years after the disclosure, Claire was standing in a grocery store checkout line when she saw a woman who, from behind, had the same haircut as the person her husband had been involved with. Her chest had constricted first, and her hands had gone cold and she was suddenly, unreasonably, fighting back tears in front of a conveyor belt of cereal and yogurt.

It passed. It always passed, faster than it used to. She paid for her groceries, walked to her car, and sat for a few minutes before driving home. She and Daniel had done the work. Two years of couples therapy. One year of individual work. Hard conversations she had not known she was capable of having. A marriage that was, by most honest measures, more present and more honest than the one that had preceded the crisis. She did not regret having stayed.

And yet.

The woman in the checkout line. The anniversary of the discovery date, which she still felt in her body even when her mind had moved past it. The way a particular song could return her, involuntarily, to the worst night of her life. She had thought, somewhere in the second year of recovery, that she would eventually reach a place where these things simply stopped. She was learning, this was not how it worked.

She was not broken. She had healed in ways she could document. What she was learning to make peace with was the recognition that healing and absence-of-all-effects are not the same thing. And that the effects that remained were not evidence that the work had failed. They were the honest shape of having survived something significant.

Evan

About a year after the divorce was final, Evan was sitting in a faculty meeting when something caught his attention.

One of his teachers was explaining why a recent project had not delivered what she had promised. She was not explaining fully, he could hear it, the selective accounting, the omissions shaped to soften the narrative. It was a familiar kind. He could track the contours of it. He had become, in the past two years, someone who noticed the particular shape of incomplete accounts.

What he had not expected was the physical response: a tightening in his chest that was out of proportion to a faculty meeting. His heart rate elevated slightly. He was aware of it the way he had learned to be aware of the waves, the body's memory arriving at moments the mind had deemed finished.

He had thought, after he left the marriage, that the hypervigilance would ease. In some ways it had. He was sleeping. He was not replaying timelines at two in the morning. The acute phase had passed in the way his therapist had told him it would pass: gradually, unevenly, with occasional reversals that were not evidence of failure.

But the calibration remained. His instrument for detecting the gap between what someone said and what was true had been, he understood now, permanently adjusted. That was not the same as being broken. His therapist had offered him a reframe he had resisted for months before he could hold it: that what felt like a wound in his perceptual system was, from a different angle, a clarification. He had always been a person who read situations carefully. He was now a person who read them more accurately.

He would not have chosen this accuracy. But it was his, and it was not going away, and there were worse things than being a person who noticed what was actually happening in a room.

The teacher finished her explanation. He asked two questions. She answered them honestly, he thought, or more honestly than she had intended at the start.

The meeting continued.

****

The repair chapters of this book have described what the work of recovery from betrayal looks like: the accountability and truth-telling that constitute the Atone phase, the emotional reconnection of Attune, the deliberate construction of a renewed relationship that is the work of the Attach phase. These are documented processes, and for couples who do this work with sustained honesty and support, the outcomes are encouraging.

This chapter addresses something that the repair framework does not fully capture: the reality that betrayal leaves effects that persist beyond the crisis, beyond the acute treatment phase, and in many cases into the long-term fabric of a person's life. These effects are not signs of incomplete healing or failure to forgive. They are the natural, well-documented residue of having experienced a serious relational trauma. Understanding them clearly, rather than being surprised or frightened by them, is one of the most useful things a person in later-stage recovery can do.

This chapter is not pessimistic. It does not suggest that recovery is impossible or that the effects of betrayal inevitably define a person's future. But it refuses the understandable but ultimately unhelpful narrative that says: if you have done the work, you will reach a point where it no longer affects you. Some people get very close to that point. Most do not reach it entirely. And the expectation that they should can itself become a source of distress, a new layer of failure added on top of what was already hard enough. What follows is an honest account of what lingers, why it lingers, and what it means to carry it well.

Anniversary Reactions and Unexpected Triggers

Among the most commonly reported long-term effects of betrayal trauma is the anniversary reaction: a surge of grief, anxiety, anger, or intrusive memory that occurs around dates associated with the affair. The discovery date. The date of a first lie or a conversation that was later revealed to have been a deception. Holidays that were celebrated during the period of the affair. Seasons of the year that carry association.

These reactions can occur years after the initial crisis, and they can surprise people who assumed they had moved past them. A betrayed spouse may have an objectively good year, feel stable and even grateful, and then notice in September or February that their nervous system has its own calendar. The body's memory does not organize itself by the markers of conscious recovery. It organizes itself around emotional salience and threat, and the dates on which significant harm occurred carry a stored charge that does not fully discharge even with successful treatment.

Research on trauma memory has documented this phenomenon across a range of traumatic experiences, not only relational betrayal. Van der Kolk's work on how traumatic memory is stored differently from ordinary autobiographical memory explains, in part, why sensory and temporal cues can activate a trauma response independent of a conscious decision to revisit the past (van der Kolk, 2014). The memory is not being summoned. It is being triggered, by cues that the nervous system has learned to associate with threat.

For betrayed spouses in the later stages of recovery, knowing that anniversary reactions are normal and expected is practically useful. It does not make them pleasant, but it removes the secondary distress of wondering whether their occurrence means something is wrong. They do not. They mean that the nervous system learned something about a particular time of year, and that learning does not simply erase itself because the present circumstances have changed.

Similarly, unexpected triggers are a normal feature of the long-term landscape of betrayal recovery. They tend to diminish in frequency and intensity over time. They do not uniformly disappear. People who have been through serious betrayal often describe an eventual relationship with their triggers that is less about elimination and more about recognition: I know what this is, I know where it comes from, and I know that it will pass. That is not the same as not having the trigger. It is a different relationship with it.

Anniversary reactions and unexpected triggers are not evidence that the work has failed. They are the nervous system's honest memory of something that genuinely happened.

The Changed Relationship with One's Own Perceptions

One of the most underappreciated long-term effects of betrayal is what happens to a person's relationship with their own perceptual confidence. Before the disclosure, most betrayed spouses trusted, to a reasonable degree, their read of their own life. They believed what they were told by their partner. They interpreted the relational data available to them as most people do: charitably, with normal error rates, in good faith.

The disclosure dismantles that. It reveals, often with brutal specificity, that the betrayed spouse was consistently misreading the situation, that the interpretation they had placed on countless interactions was false, that their confidence in their own perceptions was being exploited. This is not merely painful. It is epistemically destabilizing. The question that follows, How do I know what I know?, does not resolve easily, and in many cases it does not resolve fully.

Jennifer Freyd's concept of betrayal blindness helps explain the mechanism. Her research documents how people who depend on a relationship for safety and support are neurologically predisposed to suppress awareness of evidence that the relationship is dangerous, because conscious awareness of the threat would require a response that feels even more threatening to the relationship's survival (Freyd, 1996; Freyd & Birrell, 2013). This is not stupidity or weakness. It is the attachment system prioritizing relational continuity over perceptual accuracy in ways that are largely outside conscious control.

What this leaves, in the aftermath of disclosure, is not just grief and anger but a kind of epistemological scar, a reduced confidence in one's own read of reality that can persist long after the acute crisis has passed. Betrayed spouses often report, years after the affair, that they still notice themselves second-guessing interpretations that would have felt straightforward before. They wonder whether they are overreacting. They wonder whether a moment of discomfort is a trauma response or a legitimate perception of something real. The line between vigilance and paranoia, which was blurred by the deception, does not immediately become clear again.

This effect is important to name because it is invisible. No one watching a betrayed spouse navigate their daily life would necessarily know that behind ordinary functioning is an ongoing, quiet labor of perceptual self-monitoring that was not present before. It is exhausting in a way that is difficult to describe, and it is one of the costs of betrayal that tends to receive less attention than the more dramatic symptoms of the acute phase.

Recovery from this particular effect tends to be supported most effectively by two things: genuine, sustained transparency from the unfaithful partner, which provides ongoing evidence that the betrayed spouse's perceptions are accurate; and a therapeutic context in which the betrayed spouse is helped to distinguish between hypervigilance produced by trauma history and the legitimate signal that something in the present warrants attention.

Sexuality, Intimacy, and the Body's Long Memory

The long-term effects of betrayal on sexuality and physical intimacy are among the most common, and the most rarely discussed, aspects of recovery. For many betrayed spouses, sexual intimacy is complicated long after the acute crisis has passed by a set of associations and intrusive experiences that the body has not fully released.

These may include intrusive imagery during sexual activity, comparisons that arise involuntarily, a diminished sense of comfort or safety in physical vulnerability, and a relationship with one's own body that has been altered by the experience of having been, in some sense, a third party in a relationship one did not know was happening. These are not uncommon responses. They are, for many betrayed spouses, a persistent and demanding dimension of the long-term work.

Esther Perel has documented the particular complexity of sexuality in relational recovery after infidelity. Her work shows that for many couples, the period after disclosure is marked by enormous complexity in the sexual dimension of their relationship: some couples experience an increase in sexual activity, sometimes driven by reassurance-seeking or by the renewed intensity of the relational situation; others experience a complete withdrawal from physical intimacy that may last months or years. Neither response is pathological. Both are understandable, and both carry their own clinical considerations (Perel, 2017).

What is less commonly discussed is that these complications can persist, in attenuated form, for years. The body does not simply reset when the relational situation has stabilized. Sexuality involves vulnerability, and vulnerability involves trust, and trust was comprehensively damaged. Even in couples where trust has been substantially rebuilt, the sexual dimension of the relationship may carry residue that the rest of the relationship has moved past.

For betrayed spouses experiencing this, the most important reframe may be this; the persistence of these complications is not evidence that you have not healed, or that you are holding on, or that your body is failing to honor the work you have done. It is evidence that the body is honest, and that it carries the memory of what happened. Working with a therapist trained in trauma and sexuality can be especially helpful for this dimension of recovery, because it is distinct enough from the relational repair work to require its own attention.

Healing Without a Willing Partner

Much of what has been written in this book assumes the presence of a partner who is, at minimum, engaged in repair work: willing to stop the affair, willing to be honest, willing to do the therapeutic work that recovery requires. That assumption describes some readers' situations. It does not describe all of them.

Some betrayed spouses are carrying this in situations where the unfaithful partner is still actively deceiving, still minimizing, still refusing to engage with accountability or treatment. Others are in relationships where a superficial stability has been achieved without genuine repair: the behaviors have calmed, but the honesty is still partial, and the underlying patterns that allowed the affair to happen have not been meaningfully addressed. Others are now outside the marriage, either by their own choice or their partner's, navigating recovery in the absence of any relational context for the repair work described in this book. This section is for them.

The first thing to say is that healing is possible outside a context of active couples repair. Most treatment outcome studies focus on couples who present together for treatment, which means the literature's encouraging numbers describe a self-selected group in which both partners were sufficiently motivated to seek help together. They do not represent everyone.

But the individual processes that support recovery, including understanding the trauma, working with the body, building a stable internal life, processing grief, recovering perceptual confidence, and developing clarity about what happened and why, are all available to a person working on their own, with a skilled individual therapist, and in some cases in supported peer contexts with others who have experienced similar betrayals.

Healing without a willing partner is harder, and it follows a different path. It is not impossible. The work of recovery happens inside you as much as it happens between you.

What is different about recovery without a willing partner is this: the relational repair cannot happen if only one person is doing it. The trust-rebuilding processes described in Part Three require two people who are genuinely engaged. A betrayed spouse cannot do that work alone. What they can do, and what constitutes meaningful healing in this context, is different: it is the work of recovering their own stability, clarity, dignity, and capacity for a future that is not defined by what was done to them.

This includes, in time, the grief work of releasing what cannot be repaired. That grief is substantial and honest. A betrayal in a context where repair was refused or made impossible represents multiple losses: the loss of the relationship as it was, the loss of the relationship as it might have been with genuine repair, and the loss of the investment in a future that was being built on a foundation the betrayed spouse did not know was compromised. Grieving all of those layers honestly, rather than compressing them into bitterness or bypassing them into forced forgiveness, is the work that individual recovery makes possible.

Some betrayed spouses in this position will eventually form new relationships. What research on long-term effects of betrayal suggests is worth attending to: the hypervigilance, the perceptual disruption, the trust difficulty, and the intimacy complications documented in this chapter can carry forward into new relational contexts if they are not worked through rather than simply carried past (Shrout & Weigel, 2020). This is not an argument against new relationships. It is an argument for doing the internal recovery work fully enough that the next relationship, whatever form it takes, begins on honest ground.

Effects on Future Relationships

Whether a betrayed spouse stays in the marriage, leaves it, or is still deciding, the research on long-term effects is consistent on one point: the experience of being betrayed changes how a person relates to intimacy and trust in ways that persist beyond the original relationship. This is not a permanent sentence. It is a description of something that requires active attention rather than passive resolution.

The most commonly reported effects on future or subsequent relationships include: difficulty trusting a new partner's honesty even in the absence of evidence for concern; hypervigilance to behavioral signals that were present but unrecognized before the previous disclosure; a reduced tolerance for relational ambiguity; and a heightened sensitivity to changes in a partner's emotional availability that may or may not correlate with actual risk.

These effects can be understood as the threat-response system doing what it was designed to do: generalizing from one significant threat experience to protect against future threats of the same kind. In this sense, they are adaptive. The nervous system learned something real and is applying it. The problem arises when the application is too broad, when the calibration based on past threat is not appropriately updated to account for a present situation that is substantively different.

Russell, Baker, and McNulty's research on attachment insecurity and infidelity found that the experience of betrayal, particularly in people with existing anxious attachment tendencies, can deepen those tendencies in ways that require its own therapeutic attention to address (Russell et al., 2013). The intervention that most consistently supports recalibration in this area combines individual trauma work, processing the original betrayal thoroughly enough that its signal value is reduced, with relational experience in a new context that provides repeated evidence that the threat mapping does not apply.

This is slow work. People who have experienced serious betrayal and are in new relationships often describe a recurring internal negotiation: the awareness that a particular response is coming from the past rather than the present, and the ongoing effort to maintain that distinction under the pressure of emotional activation. Over time, with good support and a relational environment that earns trust consistently, this negotiation becomes less effortful. It does not always become unnecessary.

What helps most is not the absence of triggers in a new relational context. That is rarely available. What helps is a new partner who is patient, honest, and able to tolerate the kind of relational attention that betrayal recovery requires, and a betrayed spouse who is doing their own work rather than outsourcing the management of their past to the new relationship.

The Question of Forgiveness

No topic in affair recovery carries more confused expectations and more potential for harm than forgiveness. It is treated, in many cultural and religious contexts, as the marker of completed healing: if you have truly healed, you will forgive; if you have forgiven, you will no longer suffer. Neither of these claims is accurate, and both can do significant damage.

The definition of forgiveness matters here more than it does in most discussions because different definitions produce entirely different expectations. At one end of the spectrum, forgiveness is treated as a relational act: a declaration, offered to the offending partner, that what was done is no longer being held against them. At the other end, forgiveness is treated as an internal process, something the betrayed spouse does for themselves, independent of what the offending partner does or does not do, and independent of whether the relationship continues. These are genuinely different things and conflating them produces a great deal of unnecessary suffering.

Robert Enright's research on forgiveness as a therapeutic process makes this distinction carefully. His model identifies forgiveness as primarily an internal shift in the betrayed person's relationship to the wrong that was done: a release of the emotional burden of resentment, not for the offender's benefit but for the forgiver's. This does not require reconciliation. It does not require trust. It does not require the restoration of the relationship. It can happen, and in some cases can only fully happen, outside the relational context where the harm occurred (Enright & Fitzgibbons, 2015).

Everett Worthington's work on forgiveness and health adds a useful dimension: the research consistently finds that the internal process of forgiveness is associated with measurable improvements in physical and psychological health for the person doing the forgiving (Worthington et al., 2007). This finding has been replicated across multiple studies and cultural contexts. But it also consistently shows that this process takes time, that it is not linear, and that it cannot be produced on demand.

Let this be said without qualification: you are not required to forgive on any particular timeline, and you are not required to forgive in a way that restores the relationship or removes the right to establish consequences. Forgiveness, understood as an internal release of resentment, can coexist with clear-eyed assessment of what happened, with appropriate protective decisions, and with ongoing grief. It is not the end of feeling. It is a shift in the relationship to what was felt. To think of it from Glass' perspective, forgiveness is opening a window towards restoration.

Some people find that forgiveness comes, slowly and imperfectly, as the other dimensions of recovery proceed. Some find that it arrives as a deliberate decision, made in one deliberate moment, that does not eliminate the pain but changes its quality. Some are still working toward it years after the betrayal. All of these are honest experiences, and none of them is evidence of failure.

Forgiveness is not the last step in healing, after which everything is resolved. It is one thread in a larger work, and it tends to arrive in its own time, not on the schedule others assign to it.

What It Means to Carry It Well

There is a version of recovery that the clinical literature rarely describes well, because the outcomes research is largely organized around the absence of symptoms: reduced hypervigilance, reduced intrusion, improved relationship satisfaction, restored trust. These are important outcomes, and they are worth working toward.

But there is another version of recovery that deserves its own name, and that is the capacity to carry what remains with a certain quality of presence and intention. Not the absence of effects, but a relationship with those effects that is steady rather than frightened, honest rather than ashamed, and organized around living forward rather than being held back.

This is not a consolation prize for people who did not fully heal. It is a genuine form of wellness that is available to people who have been through significant trauma and have done the work that recovery requires. The work changes what the effects can do to you, even when it does not eliminate the effects entirely.

Post-traumatic growth research, developed primarily by Richard Tedeschi and Lawrence Calhoun, has documented that a substantial proportion of people who experience severe trauma, including relational trauma, report not only recovery but substantive positive change in dimensions of their life that were not present or as developed before the traumatic experience (Tedeschi & Calhoun, 2004). These changes include increased personal strength, greater appreciation for relationships, a deepened sense of what matters, and in some cases a revised understanding of one's own capacities.

The post-traumatic growth research requires careful handling. It is not a promise that suffering produces guaranteed benefit, or that the absence of reported growth means the work was insufficient. Not everyone experiences these changes. Some experience partial versions of them. And the research is clear that positive change and ongoing distress can coexist: finding meaning in what happened does not make what happened acceptable, or eliminate the grief, or remove the legitimate anger at the person who caused the harm.

What the research does offer is this: the picture of the person who has been through betrayal and come out the other side is not always and only a picture of damage. Some people arrive, after the full arc of recovery, with a more honest relationship to their own interior life, a more discerning approach to intimacy, and a set of capacities, including the capacity for tolerating pain, for naming difficult truths, for choosing deliberately rather than habitually, that they did not have before.

Carrying the effects well looks different for different people. For some, it means having developed a stable language for their anniversary reactions: knowing they are coming, naming them when they arrive, and not building a story of failure around the fact that they appeared. For others, it means having found a version of their perceptual confidence that is more realistic than the one they had before, less naive but not chronically suspicious. For others, it means having reached a place where the question of forgiveness has become something they are actively in a relationship with: not finished, but no longer resisted.

A Reflection: Lament as a Spiritual Practice, Not a Phase

How long, Lord? Will you forget me forever?
How long will you hide your face from me?
How long must I wrestle with my thoughts
and day after day have sorrow in my heart?
Psalm 13:1-2 (NIV)

There is a widespread expectation, in many faith communities, that grief has a proper ending: a moment of release, a prayer answered, a peace that arrives and settles. The lament tradition in Scripture challenges this expectation at its foundation.

The psalms of lament, and there are more of them than there are psalms of praise, are not the prayers of people in transition on their way to a better feeling. They are the prayers of people who are fully inside their suffering, with no resolution in sight, bringing the honest contents of their interior life to God without cosmetic adjustment. The Psalmist in Psalm 13 does not end with resolution. He ends with a declaration of trust that does not eliminate the complaint. The grief that preceded that declaration has not been retracted. It is part of the prayer, not a prelude to it.

Walter Brueggemann (1984), whose scholarship on the psalms of lament has shaped how many readers understand this genre, argues that the suppression of lament in faith communities is not a sign of spiritual maturity but of spiritual poverty. When the honest expression of suffering is silenced in the name of faith, what is lost is not merely the comfort of being heard. What is lost is a distinct kind of encounter with a God who invites that honesty. The lament tradition suggests that the God of the psalms is not one who requires the management of suffering before being approached. The full and unedited version of what the Psalmist is carrying is precisely what is welcomed.

For betrayed spouses who carry a faith, the lament tradition offers something that the clinical framework, for all its practical value, does not; the theological permission to remain in honest grief without it constituting a failure of trust or belief. The anniversary reaction that surfaces three years after disclosure is not, from this perspective, a spiritual problem to be overcome. It may be an invitation to pray the honest thing again, to bring the body's memory and the heart's grief to the same place the Psalmist brought them.

This is different from being stuck. Lament brought honestly to God, rather than rehearsed as a form of bitterness or self-pity, tends to move, not toward the elimination of grief but toward a relationship with grief that is held within something larger than the grief itself. The Psalmist moves, within the space of a single poem, from anguished question to trust. Not because the circumstances changed, but because the complaint was made honestly, and in that honesty something shifted.

Willard's (2002) description of spiritual formation as the gradual transformation of the whole person, not just beliefs and behaviors but the body, the emotions, the will, the social relations, has direct resonance at this stage of recovery. The effects that linger after betrayal are not obstacles to that formation. They are, in many cases, the precise terrain on which it occurs. Learning to carry grief with honesty and without shame, learning to bring the body's memory to a God who is not afraid of it, learning to wait without certainty for something that is not yet visible, these are not small spiritual accomplishments. They are the long work of a formed interior life.

For readers who do not locate themselves within a defined faith tradition, the same movement is available in secular forms: the honest acknowledgment that some things are carried rather than resolved, the development of a relationship with what remains that is characterized by presence rather than avoidance, and the slow discovery that carrying a wound with integrity is itself a form of wholeness.

Looking Ahead

The chapter that follows, the final chapter of this book, addresses the question that this one has been approaching from a distance: what does it mean to live forward? Not as a general aspiration but as an honest account of what the people who have been through the full arc of betrayal recovery carry into their futures, what they have lost, what they have found, and what the path ahead might look like depending on where they are standing now.

The lingering effects described in this chapter are not a conclusion. They are a landscape, and a landscape can be inhabited. The remaining work is not the elimination of everything the betrayal left behind. It is the development of a life that is honestly organized in relation to those effects: neither in denial of them nor defined entirely by them.

That is a life that is available. It does not look the same for everyone. But for the people who have done the work described in this book, it is not merely possible. It is what the work was for.

References

Brueggemann, W. (1984). *The message of the Psalms: A theological commentary*. Augsburg.

Enright, R. D., & Fitzgibbons, R. P. (2015). *Forgiveness therapy: An empirical guide for resolving anger and restoring hope*. American Psychological Association.

Freyd, J. J. (1996). *Betrayal trauma: The logic of forgetting childhood abuse*. Harvard University Press.

Freyd, J. J., & Birrell, P. (2013). *Blind to betrayal: Why we fool ourselves we aren't being fooled*. Wiley.

Perel, E. (2017). *The state of affairs: Rethinking infidelity.* Harper.

Russell, V. M., Baker, L. R., & McNulty, J. K. (2013). Attachment insecurity and infidelity in marriage: Do studies of dating relationships really inform us about marriage? *Journal of Family Psychology*, 27(2), 242–251. https://doi.org/10.1037/a0031607

Shrout, M. R., & Weigel, D. J. (2020). Infidelity's aftermath: Appraisals, mental health, and health-compromising behaviors following a partner's infidelity. *Journal of Social and Personal Relationships*, 37(5), 1503–1524.

Tedeschi, R. G., & Calhoun, L. G. (2004). Posttraumatic growth: Conceptual foundations and empirical evidence. *Psychological Inquiry*, 15(1), 1–18. https://doi.org/10.1207/s15327965pli1501_01

van der Kolk, B. A. (2014). *The body keeps the score: Brain, mind, and body in the healing of trauma.* Viking.

Willard, D. (2002). *Renovation of the heart: Putting on the character of Christ.* NavPress.

Worthington, E. L., Jr., Witvliet, C. V. O., Pietrini, P., & Miller, A. J. (2007). Forgiveness, health, and well-being: A review of evidence for emotional versus decisional forgiveness, dispositional forgiveness, and reduced unforgiveness. *Journal of Behavioral Medicine*, 30(4), 291–302. https://doi.org/10.1007/s10865-007-9105-8

Chapter Eleven: Living Forward

"You don't get your old life back. But you can, with time and honest effort, build a life that is genuinely worth living. Those are not the same thing. The second one may be harder to want, at first. It is also more real."

— composite, from a conversation about recovery after five years

At some point, if the work described in this book has been done, the crisis becomes history. Not ancient history. Not forgotten history. But history nonetheless; a chapter that has a beginning, a middle, and, however unevenly, an end. The question that remains is not whether the betrayal happened. It is what kind of person you are becoming in the aftermath of it, and what kind of life is being built from here.

That question has a serious answer, not a sentimental one, not a formulaic one. A serious answer takes into account what was actually lost, what has been durably rebuilt or set down, and what the path forward looks like from where you are standing, which is not the same place for everyone who reaches this chapter.

Some readers who arrive here have spent years in recovery with a partner who did the work. Others arrive having left a marriage and rebuilt something on their own terms. Some are further from the initial wound than they expected to be at this point; others feel closer to it than they wish they did. A few have made peace with outcomes they once thought would be unbearable. None of them arrived here by the same route, and none of them are going to the same destination.

What this chapter offers is not a promised outcome. It is an account of what living forward involves: what it means to move through the world after betrayal, what healing looks like at different distances from the wound, what the research says about long-term recovery, what faith offers for people who locate themselves there, and what the work of building a future entails for three distinct groups of readers: those who are rebuilding together, those who are rebuilding alone, and those who are still somewhere in between.

What Recovery Does and Does Not Mean

One of the most persistent misconceptions about affair recovery is that it has a clear endpoint: a state in which the betrayal no longer affects the person who was harmed. This misconception does not match the research, and it does not match the lived experience of people who have been through it.

Recovery, in the clinical literature, is better described as a reorganization than an erasure. The research of Snyder, Baucom, and Gordon, whose Forgiveness and Reconciliation through Experiencing Empathy (FREE) model has produced some of the most reliable long-term data in this area, suggests that couples who successfully recover from infidelity do not arrive at a place where the affair is as if it never happened. What they arrive at, in the most successful cases, is a place where the affair is integrated into the shared narrative of the relationship in a way that no longer dominates it. The wound becomes part of the story. It is not the whole story (Snyder, Baucom, & Gordon, 2007).

That distinction matters because it resets expectations. Couples who expect to arrive at total restoration, as if the earlier version of their relationship has been fully recovered, tend to measure their progress against an impossible standard. Couples who understand that they are building something new, something that includes an honest relationship to what happened, tend to report higher satisfaction at the two- and five-year marks than those who pursue the erasure model.

For individual betrayed spouses, the same principle applies. Recovery does not mean returning to the person you were before discovery. That person lived in a settled web of assumptions about their partner, their marriage, and their own safety in the world. Some of those assumptions were not accurate. Returning to them is not possible, and it may not even be desirable. What is possible is becoming someone who has absorbed a serious blow to their sense of the world and found, gradually, that they are still standing. That is not a small thing. It is, in fact, one of the more substantial achievements available to a human being.

Three Kinds of Forward

Where you go from here depends considerably on where you are standing right now. The following sections address three distinct situations. These are not rankings. They are not moral categories. They are simply different terrains, each of which presents different challenges and different resources.

Situation One: Rebuilding Together

For couples who have worked through the Atone, Attune, and Attach phases and who have arrived at something that looks like a rebuilt partnership, the task of living forward involves maintaining what was hard-won. Trust that has been rebuilt is not self-sustaining. Like a relationship in general, it requires ongoing tending.

What does tending look like at the five-year mark? Research by Gordon, Baucom, and Snyder suggests that couples who maintain high relationship satisfaction after affair recovery share several characteristics. They continue to practice transparency, not as a form of surveillance but as a real relational value. They have developed a shared narrative of what happened and why that is honest without being permanently destabilizing. They turn toward each other during stress rather than becoming isolated or adversarial. And they have, in most cases, both done meaningful individual work alongside the couples work: therapy, reflection, or some other process of becoming more fully themselves (Gordon, Baucom, & Snyder, 2004).

One thing the research is consistent about is that the rebuilt relationship, when it is rebuilt, tends to be more honest than the one that existed before the affair. This is not an endorsement of affairs as catalysts for growth; the harm they produce is real and not worth the cost. But it is an observation that many couples who do the full work of repair describe a relational depth and directness after recovery that they did not have before the crisis. The crisis forced conversations that comfort had made avoidable. The question of whether the relationship was worth saving required each partner to examine what they wanted, what they had been settling for, and what they were capable of offering.

For the betrayed spouse in this situation, living forward includes a piece of ongoing self-tending that is easy to overlook: the continued maintenance of their own recovery work independent of the relationship's health. The quality of the rebuilt partnership does not eliminate the individual work that the betrayal created. Anniversary reactions will still arrive. Triggers will still occur, though usually with decreasing intensity. The capacity to name these experiences without building a crisis around them is a skill that continues to develop over time, not one that arrives at a threshold and stops.

Trust, once rebuilt, is not fragile in the way it was in the early months after discovery. But it remains a living thing. It grows with continued tending and erodes with neglect. The couples who maintain the highest satisfaction at the ten-year mark are the ones who have not treated rebuilt trust as a conclusion but as an ongoing practice.

Situation Two: Rebuilding Alone

Not every person who needed this book is still in the marriage. Some readers left in the early weeks, when the scale of the deception made staying feel impossible. Others stayed through years of recovery work before reaching a point where they could see, clearly and without excessive self-blame, that the relationship did not have what it needed to survive. A few found that their partner chose to leave despite their own willingness to try.

Wherever the departure point was, the work of living forward after a marriage ends in the wake of infidelity has features that distinguish it from divorce in the absence of betrayal. Betrayal divorce tends to carry a distinct set of emotional residues: not only grief at the loss of the relationship but a more acutely relational wound, a disruption in the capacity to trust the accuracy of one's own perceptions, and sometimes a lingering shame that attaches not to anything the betrayed spouse did but to the fact of having been deceived.

Shirley Glass observed, in her clinical work with affair recovery, that the betrayed spouse's sense of their own judgment is frequently one of the last things to heal (Glass, 2003). Having trusted someone who was not trustworthy does not mean the betrayed spouse was foolish. It means they were human. But the mind does not always make that distinction automatically, and many people who leave a marriage after infidelity carry, for a while, a background question about whether they will be able to read another person accurately.

The research on betrayal trauma, and specifically Jennifer Freyd's work on betrayal blindness, helps explain why this happens without making it inevitable. The mechanism of betrayal blindness, by which the betrayed partner suppressed or minimized awareness of suspicious information in order to preserve an attachment relationship that felt necessary for survival, is a survival response, not a character flaw. Understanding that mechanism does not immediately restore perceptual confidence, but it provides a framework that can eventually support the recovery of trust in one's own perceptions (Freyd, 1996; Freyd & Birrell, 2013). Van der

Kolk's account of how trauma reorganizes the nervous system at the level of perception and threat-response provides additional grounding for this phenomenon: the body's encoded vigilance does not simply reset because the cognitive understanding has been corrected (van der Kolk, 2014).

Living forward alone also involves another challenge: what to do with the feelings about the former partner. Anger is often the most immediate. Grief is typically not far behind. Many people who leave a marriage after infidelity find that their grief is complicated by the way the person they are grieving contributed to their suffering. The marriage that ended was not a marriage without history; it contained years of genuine attachment, real experiences of love, and shared life that is worth mourning regardless of how the marriage ended. The complication of that grief, the feeling of being allowed and not allowed to be sad at the same time, is something that good grief work, whether with a therapist or in a supported grief process, can help untangle.

What many people discover, at some distance from the marriage, is that they are more intact than they feared they would be. Not untouched. Not unmarked. But more intact. The capacity they were afraid the betrayal had permanently damaged, their ability to be fully present in a relationship, their capacity for trust, their sense of their own worth in the context of intimacy tends to be more recoverable than the early period of trauma suggested. This is not guaranteed, and it is not quick. But the research on post-traumatic growth suggests that the experience of surviving a serious relational injury can, in the right conditions and with adequate support, produce a more clarified and sometimes deepened sense of self and what one wants from a relationship (Tedeschi & Calhoun, 2004).

For readers who are rebuilding alone and who are wondering about future relationships: the question of when and whether to trust again is not one that has a single answer. What the research and clinical experience both suggest is that the quality of one's own recovery work is a better predictor of readiness than the amount of time elapsed. People who have done real work with their own trauma responses, their attachment patterns, and the dynamics the previous relationship held tend to bring more clarity and more self-knowledge to subsequent relationships. They also tend, in the best cases, to bring a more honest set of expectations: less idealization, more realism, and a greater capacity to name what they need and what they will not accept.

Situation Three: Still in Between

Some readers who reach this chapter have not arrived at either of the previous situations. They are still somewhere in the middle: the marriage technically intact but not yet restored, the decision to stay or leave still unresolved, the partner still not fully accountable, the recovery still incomplete. They have been doing their own work. They are not where they started. But they are not where they hoped to be by now.

Pauline Boss, whose research on ambiguous loss describes the distinct suffering of grief that has no clear object or resolution, would recognize this terrain immediately, a relationship that has not ended but cannot yet be called restored, a loss that cannot be fully mourned because it is not yet fully named (Boss, 1999). This is a legitimate place to be, and it warrants acknowledgment rather than pressure. Not every recovery moves at the same pace. Not every partner comes fully online at the same time. Life has a way of interrupting recovery work: illness, job loss, children's crises, financial strain. The disruptions that extend a timeline are not always signs of failure. Sometimes they are just the conditions under which real human beings are doing real work.

What is worth attending to, if you are in this situation, is the difference between a recovery that is genuinely in process and a stall that has become a way of avoiding a harder decision. Those two things can look similar from the outside and even from the inside. The distinguishing features are not always easy to name, but a few markers tend to appear consistently in the research and in clinical experience.

A recovery that is genuinely in process, even a slow one, tends to show some movement: incremental increases in transparency, moments of genuine attunement that were not there six months ago, some shift in the partner's capacity to take responsibility without deflection. A stall that has become avoidance tends to show stasis: the same conversations happening with the same outcomes, the same level of accountability from the unfaithful partner, the same quality of connection, and a shared agreement, often unspoken, to not push on the things that are not moving.

If you are in the second category, the honest question is not whether you are doing enough recovery work. It is whether the conditions for recovery are present. Safety, honesty, genuine remorse, and a partner who is doing their own work are not bonuses. They are the floor. A recovery that is attempted without them is not a slow recovery. It is a different situation, and it may require a different kind of decision.

If you are genuinely uncertain which category describes your situation, that uncertainty is itself information. A trusted therapist, and ideally one with training in affair recovery, is probably the most useful resource at this juncture. Not because you cannot think clearly, but because thinking clearly about a situation you are living inside of is considerably harder than thinking clearly about almost any other kind of problem, and a skilled clinician can offer perspective that proximity makes impossible.

The Question of Forgiveness, Revisited

Forgiveness returns here at the end because it is one of the most frequently misunderstood dimensions of affair recovery, and because where you stand with it at this stage of the work matters.

The research on forgiveness distinguishes between two forms: decisional forgiveness, which is a choice to relinquish the right to punish and to recommit to behaving benevolently toward the person who caused harm, and emotional forgiveness, which is the actual internal shift in which negative feelings toward the offender are replaced by more neutral or positive ones (Enright & Fitzgibbons, 2015; Worthington, Witvliet, Pietrini, & Miller, 2007). These two forms of forgiveness do not arrive together, and they are not equally within voluntary control.

Decisional forgiveness is available to most people who choose it, and the research consistently links it to better health outcomes for the person who forgives, independent of what the offending partner does in response. Emotional forgiveness, by contrast, tends to come gradually and in fits and starts, often over years, and it is not something that can be produced on demand or accelerated by willpower.

What is important to say here is that forgiveness, in either form, is not a requirement for your healing. Some people who have done deep recovery work and who are living forward have not arrived at what they would call forgiveness of their former or current partner. They have arrived at something closer to what the research sometimes calls acceptance; a relationship with what happened that is no longer characterized primarily by active resentment, even if it has not reached the warmer forms of release. That is not a failure. It is a legitimate place to land.

Forgiveness is not, finally, a restoration of trust. Trust is rebuilt through behavior, over time, in the presence of consistent honesty. Forgiveness is an internal orientation. Offering one does not produce the other and expecting them to arrive together sets up a confusion that can prolong suffering rather than relieving it.

For people rebuilding a marriage together, the research suggests that emotional forgiveness tends to develop alongside, rather than before, actual repair. It is less a precondition than a byproduct of real relational work on both sides. For people rebuilding alone, forgiveness of the former partner, if it comes, tends to come later and often without the former partner's participation. It arrives, when it arrives, as a gift to the self, a releasing of a weight that has been carried long enough. Neither timeline is wrong. Both are real.

What You Now Know

There is a kind of knowledge that comes only from having survived something hard. It is not the knowledge you would have chosen. It is not knowledge that required a crisis to acquire. But it is yours, and it is real, and it is not nothing.

People who have done serious recovery work after betrayal frequently describe a shift in their relationship to certain experiences that they could not have articulated before. They have a more accurate sense of what they need in a relationship and what they were previously willing to settle for. They have a more practiced ability to name their own emotional states, because they have had to name very difficult ones. They have a more realistic relationship to the complexity of other people: less likely to idealize, less likely to assume that a convincing surface means an honest interior, more willing to pay attention to the details that do not add up.

They also frequently describe a more honest relationship to their own limitations. Having been hurt in a profound way tends to create at least some capacity for reckoning with the ways in which they themselves are imperfect partners, imperfect people. This does not mean blaming themselves for the affair. It means that the kind of deep self-examination that affair recovery at its best requires can produce a more truthful and more grounded self-understanding than the one that existed before.

None of this is worth what it cost. Let that stand clearly. The knowledge and the growth that sometimes emerge from serious suffering are real, but they are not a justification for the suffering, and they do not require gratitude to the event that produced them. What they require is honest acknowledgment.

You know things you did not know before. Some of them you wish you did not know. Some of them, at this distance, you are quietly glad you know. Most of them are simply yours now, part of the interior landscape of a person who has been through something and come out the other side of it still recognizable as themselves.

* * *

Claire and Evan: A Final View

Claire, whose story opened this book, is forty-three. It has been four years since the morning she found the emails that changed everything. She and her husband, Daniel, are still married. She does not describe the marriage they have now as a continuation of the one they had. She describes it as a different marriage with the same two people, or perhaps with two people who have each become someone slightly different.

The first year was the hardest year of her life. She did not have language for that at the time; she only had the day in front of her. She found a therapist in the fourth month, after a period of trying to manage on her own that she now describes as survivable but not sustainable. The therapy helped her understand what her nervous system was doing and why. It helped her stop interpreting her own reactions as weakness.

Daniel came into therapy with her, eventually, and then began doing his own individual work as well, which she did not ask for but which she believes made the difference. She can tell when he is working and when he is managing. There is a difference, and she has become reliably able to see it. That discernment is something she did not have four years ago. She is not sure she would trade it now, although she is also clear-eyed about what it cost her.

She still has anniversary reactions. They are not what they were. In the first year, they were immersive; they pulled her back into the day of discovery with a vividness that felt almost physical. Now they arrive more like weather: she can see them coming, she can name them when they are present, and she knows from experience that they pass. She no longer takes them as evidence that something is wrong with the recovery. She takes them as evidence that something happened. There is a difference between those two readings, and that difference has taken her years to inhabit rather than just understand.

She is glad she stayed. She is not certain she would make the same decision again in different circumstances, which is a complicated thing to hold alongside the gladness. She holds it.

* * *

Evan, whose composite voice has appeared in several chapters, is fifty-one. He left his marriage in the second year after discovery. The decision took longer than it should have and shorter than it felt. His former wife, Amber, had not, by the end of the second year, reached a place of genuine accountability; the partial disclosures had continued, and the story had kept changing in ways that made it impossible for him to calibrate what was true.

He does not describe the divorce as the right decision in the way that a vindication might feel. He describes it as the only decision that was available to him in the conditions that existed. He spent a year in individual therapy after the divorce was finalized, doing the work he had started during the marriage. He is now in a relationship with someone he has known for two years. He describes that relationship as the most honest one he has ever been in, and he is fairly direct about why: he has become someone who will not leave important things unnamed. That is not a gift he would have chosen. But it is a gift, and he knows it.

A Reflection: The Ground That Holds

"I lift my eyes to the mountains -- where does my help come from? My help comes from the Lord, the Maker of heaven and earth."
— Psalm 121:1-2 (NIV)

There is a moment that many people describe, somewhere in the middle distance from the original wound, when they realize that the ground has not entirely disappeared. They have been carrying that fear for a long time: that the earth beneath them has been altered at its foundation by what happened, that nothing is as solid as it appeared, that they cannot trust the stability they thought they were standing on. The moment does not arrive with certainty or with complete resolution. But something shifts. The ground that is holding them turns out to be more real than the ground they lost.

For those who locate themselves within a faith tradition, that ground has a name and a history. It is not the ground of a perfect marriage or an untroubled life. It is the ground of a God who, in the language of the lament psalms, is addressed from inside suffering without being required to first resolve the suffering before being approached. The Psalmist in Psalm 121 lifts his eyes to the mountains. He does not do so because the mountains have proven safe or because the journey ahead is clearly mapped. He does so because the help that is available does not depend on the terrain.

Dallas Willard's understanding of spiritual formation as the gradual and whole-person renovation of the interior life suggests that the work of recovery, at its deepest level, is not separate from the work of becoming. The suffering that affair recovery requires, the sustained attention to one's own interior, the reckoning with what one genuinely values and what one is genuinely willing to do, the development of the capacity to be honest under pressure and gracious under strain these are not obstacles to spiritual formation. In the best and most difficult sense, they are occasions for it (Willard, 2002).

This does not make betrayal a spiritual opportunity that anyone should seek or be grateful for. It does not suggest that God authored the harm in order to produce growth. The theological claim is simpler and more stubborn than that: whatever has happened to you, you are not beyond the reach of a kind of formation that the harm has not ultimately prevented.

Walter Brueggemann's account of the lament tradition insists that the language of complaint, of honest sorrow addressed to a God who is large enough to receive it, is not a detour from faith but one of its most authentic expressions. For readers who have, during this season, brought angry or despairing or confused prayers to whatever they understand as God: those are not lesser prayers. They may be, in the lament tradition, among the most faithful ones available. The willingness to remain in relationship with a God who has not yet answered in the way you hoped, and to continue speaking honestly into that unanswered space, is itself a form of trust that does not require resolution to be real (Brueggemann, 1986).

For those who do not locate themselves within a faith tradition, the same movement toward the ground that holds has secular forms: the discovery that one's own resilience is more available than the trauma suggested, the gradual return of a capacity for presence and joy that seemed permanently foreclosed, the quiet recognition that the worst of what happened did not, in the end, take everything. The ground that holds is not always named. But it is, for many people who have done serious recovery work, eventually discovered.

A Final Word

Living forward is not a destination. It is practice, and one that looks different at six months than it does at five years. What this chapter has tried to offer is not a promised outcome but an honest account of the terrain: what the research shows, what the work requires, and what becomes possible when it is done seriously. The ground that shifted under you was real. What you are standing on now is also real — and it will hold.

References

Boss, P. (1999). *Ambiguous loss: Learning to live with unresolved grief.* Harvard University Press.

Brueggemann, W. (1984). *The message of the Psalms: A theological commentary*. Augsburg.

Brueggemann, W. (1986). The costly loss of lament. *Journal for the Study of the Old Testament*, 36, 57–71.

Enright, R. D., & Fitzgibbons, R. P. (2015). *Forgiveness therapy: An empirical guide for resolving anger and restoring hope.* American Psychological Association.

Freyd, J. J. (1996). *Betrayal trauma: The logic of forgetting childhood abuse.* Harvard University Press.

Freyd, J. J., & Birrell, P. (2013). *Blind to betrayal: Why we fool ourselves we aren't being fooled.* Wiley.

Glass, S. P. (2003). *Not "just friends": Rebuilding trust and recovering your sanity after infidelity.* Free Press.

Gordon, K. C., Baucom, D. H., & Snyder, D. K. (2004). An integrative intervention for promoting recovery from extramarital affairs. *Journal of Marital and Family Therapy,* 30(2), 213–231. https://doi.org/10.1111/j.1752-0606.2004.tb01235.x

Snyder, D. K., Baucom, D. H., & Gordon, K. C. (2007). *Getting past the affair: A program to help you cope, heal, and move on—together or apart.* Guilford Press.

Tedeschi, R. G., & Calhoun, L. G. (2004). Posttraumatic growth: Conceptual foundations and empirical evidence. *Psychological Inquiry,* 15(1), 1–18. https://doi.org/10.1207/s15327965pli1501_01

van der Kolk, B. A. (2014). *The body keeps the score: Brain, mind, and body in the healing of trauma.* Viking.

Willard, D. (2002). *Renovation of the heart: Putting on the character of Christ.* NavPress.

Worthington, E. L., Jr., Witvliet, C. V. O., Pietrini, P., & Miller, A. J. (2007). Forgiveness, health, and well-being: A review of evidence for emotional versus decisional forgiveness, dispositional forgiveness, and reduced unforgiveness. *Journal of Behavioral Medicine,* 30(4), 291–302. https://doi.org/10.1007/s10865-007-9105-8

Conclusion

You have traveled a long way through this book. If you arrived at the first chapter in the early days after discovery, disoriented, barely sleeping, moving through the hours by habit while the interior of your life was barely manageable, you may not be in that same place now. Or you may be. The distance from that place is not measured by the number of pages read. It is measured by something slower and less linear: the gradual, non-negotiable work of a nervous system recalibrating, of a self-reassembling itself around a truth it did not choose to know. Whatever distance you have covered, something has brought you to the end of this book. That is not nothing.

* * *

I have tried, across these chapters, to give you three things. The first is accurate information. What betrayal does to the attachment bond. What the body holds that the mind has not yet processed. What safety requires before repair can begin. What real atonement looks like versus what a performance of it looks like. What attunement is, what it is not, and why it matters. What the research shows about long-term recovery for couples who do this work and for individuals who do it alone. I have tried to give you a map, because navigating without one is considerably harder than it needs to be, and because the disorientation that betrayal produces is partly a crisis of information.

The second is honest company. Claire and Evan have walked with you through these pages not because their stories are more important than yours, but because the human story of what betrayal does and what recovery looks like needs faces. Composite faces, drawn from the accumulated experience of many real people, but faces nonetheless. I have tried to hold both of their paths without ranking them. Claire stayed and rebuilt. Evan left and rebuilt differently. Neither path is the right path in the abstract. Both paths are the right path when they are the path that honest conditions, good information, and genuine self-knowledge make available.

The third is a stubborn insistence on the truth that you are not done. Not done healing, not done becoming, not done discovering what this experience has made possible in you. This is not optimism as a performance. It is an empirical claim, grounded in the research on post-traumatic growth and in twenty years of clinical observation: people who do this work seriously, who refuse both the false resolution of premature forgiveness and the false resolution of permanent bitterness, tend to find themselves, at some distance from the wound, more honest about themselves and about what they need from the world than they were before. That is not compensation for the harm. It is not a justification for it. It is simply what serious work on serious suffering sometimes produces.

* * *

There are things I could not give you in a book. I could not give you the particular knowledge of your own situation that only you have access to. I could not give you the therapist who will sit with you through the middle months, the friend who will ask the right questions, the faith community that will receive your grief without flinching, the sleep that the nervous system needs to do its work. I could not speed the timeline of emotional forgiveness, which moves on its own schedule regardless of what you understand cognitively. I could not guarantee an outcome. I have tried to give you everything a book can give. The rest belongs to the specific, irreducible work of your actual life.

* * *

A word about faith, for those who inhabit it. If you have been carrying this inside a tradition that has struggled to hold it, a church community that pressed you toward quick forgiveness, a theology that made your suffering invisible, a pastor who did not know what you were carrying, your faith, at its most honest, has always had room for this. The lament psalms were not written for people in easy circumstances. The tradition of bringing unresolved suffering to God, of speaking honestly into an unanswered silence, of refusing the false resolution that would make faith look tidier than it is, that tradition is deep, and it is yours.

If you have found that this season has changed your relationship to your faith, deepened it, fractured it, sent it somewhere you do not yet fully understand that is not a sign that something has gone wrong. It is a sign that you have been somewhere real. Walter Brueggemann's observation that genuine lament is one of the most faithful postures available to a person who is suffering is not a consolation. It is a theological claim about what honesty before God looks like. You have been living inside that claim whether you named it that way or not.

* * *

Here is what we believe, after all of this. The ground that shifted when you found out what happened was real. The loss was real. The disorientation was real. The long work of finding your footing again was real. And the ground that has held you through it — whatever you have understood that ground to be — is also real.

You are still here. That is not a small thing.

The work continues. The ground holds.

That is enough to begin again.

www.ingramcontent.com/pod-product-compliance
Lightning Source LLC
LaVergne TN
LVHW010610100826
845148LV00014B/2910

* 9 7 8 1 7 3 7 2 2 3 9 2 4 *